God's Little Sticks of Dynamite!

CW01044960

by
Barrie John Kibble

A note-friendly devotional of over 400 inspirational and challenging Christian messages married to God's word to hone and bolster your faith.

<u>CONTENTS</u>

Acknowledgement

This book is dedicated to the countless God-fearing people who refused to give up on a child of God; selfless people who sacrificed their time, effort, and resources to help the writer grow in Christ and discover a forgiving, loving God of power. They showed me how to love myself and others, and they unstintingly helped me to aim and work for something better than I could ever have hoped for—to find the true purpose of life through Jesus Christ; they taught me that none of us can overcome or succeed in the Kingdom without His precious Holy Spirit. Thank you.

EDITORIAL

In God's kingdom, the author is no greater or lesser than any other person who reads the words in this little book, whether king or commoner, rich or poor. I am no 'minister-of-the-cloth' or great theologian, but a sinner saved by grace. I remain the simplest *Holy-Spirit-filled* Christian called into prophetic ministry, and everything I write is based upon my experience during fifty years of walking with the living God and His words of power—these are the only credentials I dare offer the reader.

Originally published electronically as daily readings, they have encouraged and helped many in their journey of faith. There are over 400 messages to build courage in faith in every area of life. Ponder one for a few minutes, an hour, or spread over a full day, a month, or as long as necessary. There is space below each entry for Bible study notes, with extra blank pages at the back, or for personal reflections, or a distinct word from God.

Above all, meditate, pray, and apply what God is saying through His word. Faith and works go hand in hand—neither have life without the other. I have witnessed amazing acts of God, including prayers and promises answered; miracles of healing, deliverance, and providence, souls restored, and minds and attitudes changed by His Holy Spirit. I'm not perfect, but in God's eyes I am perfect through Christ yet still being perfected for this kingdom business—and so are we all.

Take hope, for God will never abandon you. His promises, gifts, and calling are irrevocable, His love unconditional.

Simply believe.

'God's Little Sticks of Dynamite' is a simple inspirational journey into faith-growth with His precious Holy Spirit at the helm. Pray each time before you open this book, and ask the Holy Spirit to unlock the eyes and ears of your heart and soul, and then expect a divine exchange!

FORWARD

Having walked alongside Barrie in both ministry and friendship I highly recommend these short but powerful, faith-filled meditations. I have seen Barrie live these words out on a daily basis. They are not just good ideas, but wise and powerful promises and declarations from a good, gracious, and merciful God and Father who loves us unconditionally.

These words have been proven in the crucible of the author's life, and as you embrace these truths underpinned with the 'Word of God', I believe that you will likewise see them strengthen and transform your own lives.

These words are as the title says little sticks of dynamite, and they contain the dynamic power to transform your thinking, and therefore your life. The book's journal-type format allows space to add notes after each reading, so that every succinct but powerful piece becomes a place of personal encounter with God that you can return to time and time again.

I know you will be blessed and transformed as you read and meditate over so many faith-rich inspired words.

Ross Hardy—*senior Pastor of River Church Seaford, East Sussex, and founder of Beachy Head Chaplaincy Team.*

A Personal Message

The words of God are supernaturally infused with divine power. When His words strike your mind, burrow into your heart, and empower your spirit by His Spirit they bring wisdom, anointing, conviction, love, encouragement, comfort, healing, deliverance, peace, hope, character, a reason for living, and they forge an overcoming faith! Active faith is to read God's word, believe it, and then live it out. "A person is made right with God through faith." (Rom3:28)

God bless all who read this little book, and let Him keep you in His unfailing and unconditional love through faith in His amazing grace in Christ Jesus. With expectant faith, the author prays these facts, words and experiences be divinely infused with whatever God deems right and proper to convey at any given time to build up those He loves and has called by name—Jehovah Shalom.

'My sheep hear My voice, and they follow Me. And I give them eternal life, and they shall never perish; neither shall anyone snatch them out of My hand. My Father, who has given them to Me, is greater than all; and no one is able to snatch them out of My Father's hand.' (John 10:27-29)

UNCONDITIONAL LOVE

'If love is free, why do we spend all of our days trying to earn
it?'

(1) If you think no one cares or loves you, well, Christ does, and He's prepared to love you unconditionally. That's despite whatever you've done in the past, and the mistakes you're going to make. Check God's word, nowhere does it say that those who call on His name will be ignored, shunned, punished, condemned or forced to live without forgiveness, hope, and renewal. The love, peace, and joy of the Lord are yours if you want them? That's minute by minute and day by day. See with the eyes of faith and accept His miraculous gift of unconditional love. **(Deut 31:8, Ps 37:24, 55:16, Ps 91)**

(2) Sacrificial love: A woman washed Jesus' feet with an expensive oil using her hair! An utter waste in the eyes of sinners and unbelievers on the wide road to hell, yet it's another precious secret to those on the narrow path to heaven. The blinding light of sacrificial love draws sinners to Christ and exposes their darkest sins, crippling secrets, and deepest fears, and such love can break asunder the most stubborn and hard-hearted of souls, and remove the sting of death through Christ. Unconditional love saves those ignorant of hell, and she encourages and galvanises those already on the road to heaven. Ask the Father for more of His love. He'll hold nothing back from the pure of heart, from those who seek Him and love Him. **(Luke 7:36-50)**

(3) We often love conditionally, but God's love is unconditional, packed with forgiveness, and wrapped with grace. Love means accepting and forgiving people whatever the cost. Love doesn't mean we must accept what's wrong and injurious, but love should be reflected in how we handle such matters. Love rides hand in hand with forgiveness and mercy—best leave the complicated business of justice and judgement to God. The most important facets of a simple life are to love God, to love others despite themselves, and . . . to love yourself! **(1 Cor 13)**

(4) Man-made gods and idols want something impossible that ends with their disciples' misery and control. The insatiable thirsts of these gods are impossible to quench. They lord it over enslaved spirits, destroying hopes, dreams, and free will. They know nothing of love, peace, freedom, or virtue—only want, want, want. There's a living God, not made from human hands, who is pure love and desires only the best for those who seek Him.
(Ex 20:3, Lev 19:14, Ps 31:6, 106:36, 2 Cor 6:16)

Barrie Kibble

TRIALS AND TRIBULATIONS
'Only a furnace can produce pure gold.'

(5) *'Greater is He that is in you than he that is in the world.'* Tough day or month, bad news, hard times, illness, difficult job, under constant spiritual attack—your position in Christ is assured and His power in you is sealed by the Holy Spirit. You can handle anything if you turn to God's word and apply it, constantly if necessary, until you overcome and find God's peace in every circumstance. Don't forget the armour of God in Ephesians, vital tools in spiritual warfare—*if* you keep them on. This war isn't about flesh and blood, but the devil's supreme supernatural efforts to keep you from God and a life well-lived. **(1 John 4:4, Eph 6)**

(6) Do we want to fall at or jump every hurdle? Stop trying to wriggle out of life's learning curves; it makes us unapproachable, moody, miserable, apathetic, and our negative thoughts and behaviour set us up for future failures. God builds integrity and character in us through trials and tribulations. Go through them with a patient faith fat with hope. Even when life gets tough, determine to be responsible for your attitude, words, and actions. Think of others above yourself and you earn self-respect and their respect. You'll be able to face anything and anyone if you live right and let God be God in every area of your life, especially when it gets tough. Let's face the music and dance. **(James 1:2, Pet 1:6)**

(7) Father God can't be compared with any earthly father. God's faultless and constant love goes way beyond human reasoning. To love is to never stop giving. *'For God so loved the world that He gave His only begotten son.'* You have a spiritual father of love who takes pains about your every need, and He's mapped your day so you needn't worry or fuss. Spend time with Him today, and He'll father you whatever your circumstances.
(Ps 68:5, 89:26, Isa 9:6, John 3:16, 1 Cor 8:6, 2 Cor 1:3, Gal 4:6, 1 John 3:1)

(8) Unlike God's Holy Spirit, the devil can't be everywhere. The devil sends his demons to ride your back if they can find something to grab onto. Their job is simple: to smother your joy and peace, find your weaknesses, exploit them, and keep you from God; make you miserable, remind you how worthless you are and how pointless life is. Demons are dispatched to steal your faith; destroy your hopes and dreams. What are your weaknesses and fears, your habitual sins and bad attitudes? Work on these with God or they'll work on you! **(1 John 3:8, Eph 4:27, 2 Tim 2:26, 1 Pet 5:8)**

(9) Often, the devil likes to attack us immediately after a breakthrough, an answer to prayer, when we've blessed someone or been blessed, after healing or deliverance, when things are going well, or after God speaks to us. Never let your guard down. Be watchful on the walls of your spiritual life or the devil will find a crack. He'll exploit the breach and pour in temptation, despair, guilt, self-pity, pride, or unbelief. Stay alert and fight the good fight of faith. **(Eph 6:18, 1 Pet 5:8)**

(10) The devil's priority is to steal your faith, keep you blind and ignorant of God's power and the freedom of walking with Him. The devil's after those who've crossed their names out of his book and been indelibly written into God's book, and he's after them with a vengeance! If he can steal or destroy your faith, he'll make you impotent, useless to all. Stay in God's word and stand firm, for your enemy was beaten and disarmed on the cross, best you realize this truth and constantly remind the devil of it. **(1 Cor 1:18, Col 1:20, 2:14-15)**

(11) *'The Lord's arm is never short to save'* from every distress or temptation if we would but turn to Him expectantly despite our doubts and fears. Thanking Him for what He's already done in our lives draws God's ear to our troubles and spreads wide the doors to the warehouses of heaven. Faith is strengthened through praying His word, and then your faith, despite being the size of a mustard seed, bursts into flower and fruit. Are you in a fix? Earnestly seek God in the midst of trouble and expect His deliverance? **(2 Chron 20:17, Ps 32:7, Phil 1:19)**

(12) Part of growing as a Christian is tribulation. Often trouble comes from other Christians; we argue until we're blue in the face, but everyone's right and everyone has a handy Bible verse to back that up. Nothing in human reasoning is black and white. We must trust to God that He's working out our troubles for our good; we must trust in no other, for people will always fail us. *'Wait on the Lord and He will renew your strength.'* **(Ps 34:19, Isa 40:31, Rom 8:28, 2 Cor 4:17)**

(13) In the storms of life, turn your thoughts to God and utilise your faith. As an aspirin is to a headache, God's word is to life—medicine. His word is a living hope. *'Call upon the Lord in your distress and He will deliver you.'* Take your eyes off the tempest and see the impossible made possible. Peter took his eyes off Christ and sank, so keep your gaze on God. Stick in there. *'All things work together for your good if you love God and are called according to His purposes.'* **(Ps 18:6, 55:16, 118:5, Hab 3 17-19, Rom 8:28)**

(14) Today, God says, "You are His and nothing can snatch you from Him. Nothing evil can come to you that He didn't know about and wasn't ready for. Yet, when trouble comes, it won't smother your spirit or soul, or drown your love and joy. The battle is in the heavenly places, so stand firm and ride the storm." The victory is already God's. Do your bit: *'Simply believe.'* LIVE ONE DAY AT A TIME. Only do those things God has called you to do today. Stay in the word and prayer; trust in Him.
(2 Chron 14:11, Ps 37:34, Acts 17:28)

(15) *'The trial of your faith is more precious than gold.'* The refining process is 'uncomfortable', but it will save your spiritual life, strengthen your character, help you mature, and you'll always be ready for what God wants you to do. True joy and peace come out of a submissive attitude to Him who knows what's good for you. However hard it may seem for a while, don't settle for less by turning from God's best. **(2 Thess 1:4, James 1:2-4, 1 Pet 1:6)**

(16) All of us have a lot to learn about handling troubles. If you're God's child, nothing can happen to you that hasn't already passed through Him—it's your eternal soul that matters to Him. Job had to learn that lesson. Wherever you are and whatever you're going through *'God will keep you in perfect peace if your mind is stayed on Him.'* Endeavour to recognise and accept His lordship over everything, and you'll remain secure under His blessing. You may not believe it now, but hold fast, for *'all things work together for your good!'* **(Isa 26:3, Rom 8:28, Job)**

(17) If God is silent we must be growing? There are times we wonder what God's up to; the heavens are brass, and we appear to travel the dark valleys alone. God allows due season for our own good. To be stretched by God is painful while He equips us for service. If you don't know suffering, then you won't understand grace. A patient faith brings its own rewards in due time. Giving up in troubles isn't an option—people out there need us. God will speak again when He's ready, so persevere with a resolute faith. **(Job 36:15, Ps 23, Acts 5:41, Rom 5:3, 8:17, Cor 1:5, 2 Tim 3:11, 1 Pet 4:12)**

(18) Two divine and sublime promises to get you through tough situations: *'Call upon me in the day of your distress and I will deliver you'* and, *'I will keep in perfect peace whose mind is stayed on Me.'* Don't let these promises remain unread in the good book, or sit staring you in the face. Dig them out, utilize them, and learn them by heart. Own and use them as yours through your journey of prayer to praise. **(Ps 34:1, 42:5, 50:15, Isa 26:3, 50:2)**

(19) WHY ME? When illness or trouble hit we shake a fist at God and cry "why me?" Some are healed, some aren't, the mountain moves for some but not for others, and evil people flourish while the innocent suffer. We only know a fragment of His truth. We must be slow to draw conclusions, reserve our reactions to people and circumstance until we understand His greater plan for us. Hang onto God. Wait for Him. Paul suffered much, almost died, but God didn't take him home until his ministry was finished—it wasn't up to the devil, sickness, the stoning crowds, or even the Roman authorities. *'In the world you will have tribulation, but take courage for I have overcome the world.'* **(John 16:33)**

(20) Hold fast in the day of trouble. Stand firm for *'His banner over you is love.'* This is your reason to hope, the power in your faith. The great shepherd will bring you through every storm into fresh pasture and rest. Don't give up—press through, and see the salvation of your Lord and saviour. **(Song of Sol 2:4)**

(21) *'The devil meant it for evil, God meant it for good.'* We believe life must go smoothly because of our faith in God. When difficulties come, we often retreat from Him and throw out faith because it makes no logical sense that a loving, all-powerful God would allow trouble to touch His own. We need to remember Jacob's story. We need to persist in pursuing God's promises to us, staying close to Him whatever the circumstance. With the Holy Spirit guiding, we need to ride difficulties with faith through prayer. **(Gen 50:20, John 16:33)**

(22) *'Be anxious for nothing, the Father knows what you need.'* 99% of the worry thoughts that strike us never materialise. Worry drains our peace and joy, and it'll not change our circumstances one iota. Our concerns are His concerns. *'In all things by prayer and thanksgiving, cast your anxiety, cares, and concerns upon Christ.'* Trust God with all your heart, mind, and soul. Find the appropriate verses in the word of God that deal with worry and focus on them. **(Ps 94:19, 139:23, Matt 6:25-34, Phil 4:6-7)**

(23) *'No weapon formed against you shall prosper.'* Learn this verse well and use it with the power invested in you by Christ through the Holy Spirit. God's word has to be acted upon in faith for it to be effective. We say: "But will you?" Christ says: "I WILL." What's written is written. Apply God's word to every situation. Faith has to be active to work. God's promises are yours; the only condition is: FAITH IN ACTION. Face every day with hope, confidence, and courage, and let the word of God back you to the hilt. **(Isa 54:17, Matt 8:2)**

Barrie Kibble

TRUST
'Trustworthy are those who do what they say rather than those who say what they should do but don't.'

(24) *'Trust in God and lean your entire personality on Him.'* It's folly to trust in self or others to supply your every need. If you recognise and acknowledge the Lord in everything, He'll direct your paths and bless you continually. In this world, it's hard to trust anyone—but taste and see that the Lord is good and true to his word. Don't be wise in your own eyes or put faith in human reasoning—trust in the Lord. **(Ps 37:25, Prov 3:5-6, Rom 15:13)**

(25) Don't be frightened or fearful, nor dread what the days may hold. Eat only today's *manna,* and God will look after our tomorrows. Trust all to Him in faithful prayer who can keep us and all our ways, mind, flesh and bones. Through absolute child-like trust we're safe beneath His wings until He takes us home. Take Christ by the hand and walk calmly into every hour, knowing He's overcome death, the world and the devil, and He's given us power to do the same as we refuse to let fear, dread, and panic control us. **(Ps 3:6, Isa 41:10, 1 John 4:18)**

(26) Joseph was wrongly accused, yet he had no time for self-pity or thoughts of revenge during his years in prison. He considered integrity to be his human standard; his unwavering trust in God's promises and justice was his soul's hope. Held in high regard by jailor, guards, and inmates alike, he grew in stature, responsibility and wisdom to become governor of Egypt. God allowed everything at precisely the right time in Joseph's life to eventually save his entire family from death. *'God's thoughts aren't our thoughts.'* Never lose hope! **(Gen 50:20, Isa 55:8, Rom 8:28)**

(27) God takes account and invoices those who persecute or try to control you, speak falsehoods, bully you, or demand you change to suit their ambitions. Obedience to the Holy Spirit will keep you in God's perfect plan despite setbacks with people in church or the world. So trust Him; resolve to keep your eyes on your certain journey and destination with overcoming faith, hope, praise, joy, and peace. Leave the justice and vengeance business to God. You're not built nor programmed to handle retribution with perfect wisdom and fairness. God sees and weighs every heart—best keep out of it, and let Him balance the books. *'Pray for those who persecute you.'* **(Matt 5:11-44, 12:36, 1 Pet 4:5)**

(28) When facing trouble, people will trust in all else before they're willing to trust in God's word: the doctor, savings, horoscopes, others advice, the next pay cheque, the new job. Until come the day things and people fail us. God isn't put out; He waits and longs to have a deeper relationship where His children will trust in a Father who looks after every little detail, and to whom '*nothing is impossible.*' **(Matt 17:20, Luke 1:13)**

(29) Due season: A farmer sows seeds and then patiently waits with faith for a harvest. He doesn't go out after a week and dig the seeds up to see if they're growing. That's the same with God's promises. You need to sow them and then get on with your life while you wait for the harvest. Don't continually dig your seed up with negative words and so erode your faith. All you need do when the crows of doubt attack is to keep them away from the crop by confessing God's promise(s) to you.
(Gen 15:11, 2 Sam 21:10, James 5:7)

(30) Worry is simply refusing to trust God with our problems. It's not arrogant or foolhardy to say, "I'm not going to be anxious about anything today." That's a bold statement, fat with faith, and it pleases God. Jesus said, *'Don't worry,'* so we can lay EVERY problem at his feet, but we have to let go of them. It takes practice to act on God's word. We have to get into His word, learn verses by heart, and apply them to our mind when needed. Replace worry with a carefree trust in God. Try it—it's liberating! **(Matt 6:25-34)**

(31) *'DO NOT WORRY,'* is a direct command of Jesus. He means: if you belong to the God who knows and understands all things, He's now in the driver's seat of your life and you gave Him complete control. So, the command *'Don't worry'* isn't up for discussion. If you fail to believe or rest in those words, it means you'd rather steer yourself through life's storms because you don't trust the Captain or His credentials. How do you think He feels about that? **(Luke 12:1-11, 22-31)**

(32) Whenever He awoke, Jesus didn't know what He'd eat or where He'd sleep that day, but trusted His heavenly Father would provide. Jesus never turned to fleshy reasoning to sort out issues and problems. He listened to—and acted on—what his Father said. When God is at the centre of all you do and think, then worry, anxiety, and fear are replaced by hope, peace, and joy. With faith, practice makes perfect, and it's never too late to start! *'Seek you first the kingdom of God and ALL your needs WILL be added to you.'* **(Matt 6:33, 12:50, John 8:28, 14:10)**

(33) The Christian walk can reflect the excitement of shooting the rapids in a dinghy, paddling madly, or falling in and not caring. Then there's the pleasure cruiser, where you sit back and enjoy the scenery. There are times you're on a battleship and the fight is full-on, heavy guns blazing; other times, you're happy to bob gently in a side-water, resting and catching the sun, drifting a hand through still waters. Occasionally, you're in a force ten gale in a tiny rowing boat holding on for dear life—whatever happens, wherever you are . . . you're *never* alone! **(Ps 73:23, Matt 28:20)**

(34) Life's often a struggle, and we trudge from one problem to the next; misery upon misery and we want to give up. There has to be a balance between sunshine and rain, or we can't grow and can't produce a harvest. There are no true quick fixes to life's problems, but God is always close and *'He will keep your foot from being taken.'* Hang on to his hand, trust Him despite the odds—you *will* turn the corner. This is your overcoming-all-through-faith in action. **(Ps 18:17-19, 46:1, Prov 3:1-26)**

(35) It's easy to give up when everything turns to dust, but God can save and rebuild, and at just the right moment. Often, we need to look at sin in our lives, or if we've been travelling the wrong path and need to return to the cross. Maybe God is actually refining us as He did with Moses, Job, and Peter in order to strengthen our faith. God will never fail you; He'll deliver you. That's His part of the covenant, so keep your part—trust and hope in Him today despite how things look, or how you feel.
(Prov 4:27, John 15:1-25, 16:1-3)

(36) When all's falling apart, it's hard to trust God. When the devil throws all his forces against you and you want to give up, remember, live one day at a time and recall the former blessings. Has God ever failed you? *'I was young now I am old, but I have never seen the Lord's chosen forsaken.'* You are being stretched for future battles, so wait for God's trump card. Trust Him to deliver you into victory. **(Ps 37:25)**

(37) Your joy and peace aren't reliant on church or people, nor their appraisal or opinion of you. They have their place in our development, but the crucial part of living is for you to be one with God at all times. The person you ought to turn to first in any matter is God. *'Work out your own salvation with fear (reverent awe of God and hatred of sin) and trembling.'* You cannot adopt, live in, or rely on someone else's salvation. Put your trust first and foremost in God today and you'll walk upright because you're much lighter. **(Mic 6:8, Rom 8:6)**

(38) *'Set God before you at all times.'* No need to be shaken or moved, for He's always with you. Focus on Christ, and the day will go well. There may be problems or even heartache, yet you'll know and sense the presence of God. You may not understand events, but you will find God is in control, and what He doesn't explain to you at present will become clear in time. Trust God's hand to save you, and His words to comfort. **(Gen 17:1, Ps 4:1, 27:1, 56:4, Prov 11:28, 30:5, Matt 28:20, John 14:1-3, 2 Cor 3:4)**

(39) The school of knocks: We can cope with one, maybe two setbacks, but when they flood in we're quickly demoralised. We either move closer to God, or we draw away, doubt, moan, and melt into disinterest, hopelessness, and misery. It's in drawing closer to Him that we find His strength to cope in greater degrees. We only see the 'burning bush' if we're searching for it. God wants us to grow through the tough times and not shrink and wither, to trust in Him and not in our unreliable self-reliance. Look for God in the impossible. **(John 16:32-33, 1 John 4:3-5)**

(40) Are you willing to be shaped and moulded, fashioned into a vessel that the potter knows will be best for the job of life? A skilful potter can turn a lump of clay into a work of beauty, both pleasing and functional to all. It can take a lifetime to fashion us perfectly. God's amazing designs aren't meant to be locked in storerooms gathering dust, but used everyday. Despite whatever stage of workmanship you're at, stay on the wheel and talk to the master potter today. **(Isa 64:8, Jer 18:1-2, Rom 9:21)**

(41) The wilderness: We must all travel barren wastelands. People stranded in jungles or deserts perish if they don't know how to resource from the seemingly impossible. We have to survive in a world of rampant evil. God will supply our every need, but we need to know and act on His word to quench spiritual hunger and thirst. Ignorance and apathy beget spiritual death. Faith at work is the key, the source of spiritual survival and revival. Jesus was a man like us, yet He knew and applied God's word, and after 40 days in a wilderness He emerged stronger because of it!
(Prov 30:5, Matt 4:1-11)

(42) *'If you abide in me . . . many will fall around you, but not you.'* The command to abide in Him is for our protection, security, and well being in every situation. While people lose their heads about us we trust in God's saving embrace. *'For God has not given us a spirit of fear, but of love, of power, and of a sound mind.'* We must know this so that we're ready to help those who need Christ when their world falls apart. **(Ps 91, 2 Tim 1:7)**

(43) *'Do not be afraid of the arrows by day.'* How's your faith? Part of our spiritual armour is the faith-shield. A vital piece of protection, the shield repels loneliness, guilt, doubt, hopelessness, despair, rejection, and unbelief. The devil's arrows always fly, but often we let our shield drop. The shield of faith is cast from a steel mould of belief, trust, and hope. Keep your shield up, or you're going to get wounded. **(Ps 91)**

(44) *'Do not be afraid of the terror by night.'* It's awful to wake with a start in the pitch black. God doesn't just protect by day. The deal's all-in, paid in full, stamped, and filed. All outstanding debts, fears, and worries were nailed to the cross. Don't let the devil heap them back on your shoulders at some unearthly hour. That's the time to pray, to preach the devil a sermon, and to expect the Holy Spirit's comfort. *'He grants his beloved sleep.'* **(Ps 4:8, Ps 91)**

(45) *'He shall deliver you from every snare.'* But you need to walk and talk God like you need to breathe air. Remain in His blessing, and the Holy Spirit will guide your steps, keep you from harm. Recognize His gentle whisper—it takes practice. *'God's word is health to your flesh, and strength to your bones,'* and it's a sure guide through life's minefields. The devil hunts faithless Christians, apathetic souls; he sets traps for the unwary, and he knows how to utilize their weaknesses. Stick close to God! **(Ps 91, Prov 3:8)**

(46) *'In Him I trust.'* Trust is a vital tool available from God's equipment shelf. Trust and faith are often inseparable. King David as a shepherd had to kill fox, then bear, then lion before he could slay the Philistine giant! Build your trust in God through all situations whether good or bad. Fix faith-block upon rigid faith-block to withstand life's storms and the demons of hell. Trust is the hammer and nails of faith, and together they fashion 'giant killers'. *'When I am afraid, I will trust in you.'* **(Ps 56:3, Ps 91)**

(47) *'Under the shadow of God.'* If you are God's, nothing can happen to you that hasn't passed through Him. Job had to learn that valuable lesson. The shadow abides when you abide with God. At home, work, or school, through good or ill, on bus, plane, or train, up a mountain or in a cave, hospital or prison, *'He shall keep in perfect peace whose mind is stayed on Him.'* Endeavour to remain secure under His shadow. **(Ps 91, Isa 26:3, John 14:27)**

(48) *Jehovah-jireh*: God provides, and part of His provision is spiritual health. *'My cup runs over.'* If your cup is full, pour the contents into others and it'll run over again. Just as Old Testament manna rotted, if you don't use what you have it too stagnates. Today's blessing has no room for yesterday's blessing or tomorrow's. Travel the extra mile and He'll provide a well. The good shepherd leads his flock to fresh water. **(Ps 23)**

(49) *'I shall not want.'* If a child trusts its imperfect parents to supply every need, why can't we trust our perfect heavenly Father to do the same? *'If you ask for bread would He give you a stone?'* and, *'The Lord knows what you need even before you ask.'* The good shepherd provides shelter, pasture, guidance, and comfort 365 days a year. Travel light. You only need what is healthy for mind, body, spirit, and soul for earth's mission. **(Ps 23, Matt 7:7-9)**

(50) Comfort in loss: We have a God of comfort and His gift of prayer. We put both together when we hear of those suffering from grief, relations and friends of those who've lost loved ones through violence, war, accident, murder, acts of nature, disease, or sudden death. We need not know them to stand with them, but God knows them by name. *'The Lord whom you seek will suddenly come.'* **(Ps 116:5, Lam 3:22, 32, 2 Cor 1:3)**

(51) Single and anxious you'll never marry? If you've learned to trust God with the small things, why sweat the big things? He knows what's best for your life and exactly when it should happen. Many Christian marriages fail because we rush ahead of God; convinced in a moment of sheer bliss or sheer desperation that we've found Mr. or Mrs. Right. If we know God, then we trust Him to sort everything in our lives while we concentrate on taking care of His business. **(Prov 3:5, 1 Cor 2:2)**

(52) Confidence is the fruit of trusting God for the next hour, the remainder of the day, tomorrow, and the rest of your week. If the thing you fear most shall come upon you . . . get rid of it now, why wait? A bomb disposal expert is charged with dismantling a bomb, not sitting and staring at it, sweating, wondering when it will go off. Give all your problems to God and let Him turn them into victories, into faith; faith breeds trust and trust blossoms into confidence. God-confidence is more than able to provide all you need for life so you don't turn back or give up.
(Ps 20:7, 28:7, 91:2, Prov 3:5-6, Isa 50:10, Nah 1:7, Heb 4:16, 13:6, 1 John 5:14)

(53) We try to give up worrying and want to trust God as He asks, but we find the resulting void difficult to handle. There's a strange foreboding comfort in trying to control things we cannot possibly control, as if our brain really could change events that only God can determine. *'He works all things for our ultimate good.'* "But that doesn't make sense" we say—it's not supposed to. God knows the end from the beginning; our job is to simply trust Him and stop worrying. A habit needs repetition to become a habit, good or bad.
(Isa 55:8-9, Rom 8:28, Rev 21:6)

FORGIVENESS

'A painful splinter left in the finger will soon become an agonizing stake through the heart."

(54) Has someone hurt you and you don't know why, or you do know, and they haven't heard your side? Have they broken a confidence, besmirched your name, falsely accused you, abandoned or deserted you, or been downright evil. Well, before the devil makes the hurt a stronghold and teaches you to hate, to seek revenge, and poisons you with bitterness that can lead to physical and mental illness . . . give the offence to God. Quickly forgive those who hurt you whether they know or care. Until you learn to forgive at the *blink-of-an-eye*, you'll never realise God's wisdom and logic is the only way to true freedom! (Matt 6:15, 18:21-22)

(55) Forgiving those who've hurt us is often extremely difficult; the depth of unforgivingness being equal to the extent of damage. Let's not pretend or be falsely pious, nothing will change us or others until we grasp the nettle and absorb the stings. Our lives needs to move forward, not remain at the well of anger and despair, or at the brook of vengeance, for both will drown our spirit. Continually take all to God and learn that forgiveness is a repetitive act of will. Christ paid in blood to forgive us; to give me and you a second chance at life, so why let unforgivingness for past or present hurts hamstring future health, joy and peace? (Matt 6:14, 18:21-22, Col 3:13)

(56) When we refuse to forgive those who've wronged us we produce bitter fruit. We can become ill or never move forward, and the world is a sadder, darker place. Don't be fooled, our unforgivingness has no affect on those who've hurt us. Often, we must forgive the unforgivable. Yes, it takes humility, a huge dose of courage, and a tremendous act of will. Forgiveness is the antidote for unforgivingness, freeing us to live life to the full. God's justice is perfect. He knows everybody's heart. There's enough to carry in life without the extra baggage. Jesus showed us that there's no limit to forgiveness. (Matt 18:21-35)

(57) We wonder why God doesn't feel the same way about the people we dislike, those who hurt us or damage the ones we love and hold dear. It maybe frustrating when God says, *'He doesn't weigh man's agendas like we do,'* but through grace, He loves every one of his children whether they're right or wrong in human eyes. God works on all clay to fashion vessels that quickly forgive and show love to each other in order to save the lost. God is mysterious—we'd best get used to that wonderful fact. (Isa 29:16, 55:8, 1 Pet 1:7)

(58) Are you misunderstood, or have you been accused or maligned for something you never did or said? Wait upon the Lord for He'll set your innocence as a standard. He'll strengthen and help you raise the banner of truth. Don't take matters into your own hands, nor grow weary or angry at those who malign, persecute, or revile you. Pray for them instead, be lovingly patient, heap blessings upon them, forgive, and see the deliverance and judgement of the Lord. **(Rom 1:18, 12:19)**

(59) One way to bless your life and to be at peace is to learn to forgive and love others despite themselves; that's neighbours and strangers, as well as friends and family. *'Love covers a multitude of sins.'* Learn to pray for those who speak evil of you, mock, and knock you. You'll be surprised how God will turn things around to cover you with grace and favour. Do all things out of love, not revenge or self-satisfaction. **(1 Cor 13, 1 Pet 4:8)**

(60) Unforgivingness destroys us a little chunk at a time. While it may be fully justified not to forgive evil acts or words, it's an approach that only harms *us*. Unforgivingness won't affect those responsible for our hurt, anger, or misery. Let it all go, and let God heal the wounds. Unforgivingness rots the spirit and soul, and warps the heart, turns us to resentment, and ultimately to bitterness and hate. Unforgivingness can lead to all sorts of illness, depression, and behavioural problems. Talk to God—let it all go. **(Matt 6:15, 7:1-5, 18:21-22)**

(61) God will gently show us how to forgive and let go; leave justice and reparation to Him. Unlike us, He knows the hearts of people, what motivates and drives them. Meanwhile, He wants us to live free again. Our forgiveness can change us for the good; change others and situations and the world about us. Talk to God—decide to let unforgivingness go. **(Prov 16:1-7)**

Barrie Kibble

PRODIGAL STUFF
'Pigs are meant to live in pig sties, people aren't.'

(62) Have you given up on God, become disillusioned with Him? Has something awful happened, someone died, the world sucked you in and spat you out, or maybe you couldn't keep the course of faith? Have people, especially Christians, hurt or damaged your concept of Christ and true freedom? God has no favourites. He's ever faithful and never turns off the tap of love. God is always ready to forgive the repentant heart, restore the broken spirit, and heal the damaged soul. What better time to return to Him and find your purpose again. **(Joel 2:25, Luke 15:11-32, 1 John 1:9)**

(63) All of us at some time must lay our baggage at the cross and refuse to carry it another step. No one has true peace until they put themselves right with God. Then they can live life to the full—let go of themselves and live for others. If you started with Christ and fell away, know this today: '*He will never leave or abandon you, for He is faithful even when we are not.*' He may have to bring you along the hard road or through the fire, but He will restore you because He loves you too much to lose you! **(1 Thess 5:24, Heb 10:23)**

(64) Just as we go to the local waste facility and cast our rubbish, Christ's sacrifice means we can dump our millstones of fleshy junk at the foot of His cross: sin, emotional pain, fear, guilt, demons, unforgivingness, hate, etc. Take those weighty sacks to Him and be rid of them. Start life afresh; it's never too late with God, for *'His mercy, grace, and faithfulness are new every morning'*—He is quick to rescue, forgive, heal, and restore.
(Ps 55:22, Lam 3:22-24, Phil 3:13, 1 Pet 5:7)

(65) Many find Christ, and then the lust, trinkets, and fruit of the world draw them back to a self-centred life of sin excused by modern reasoning. They want and believe an outdated God ought to catch up with modern trends. Anything goes, because everyone else does it. Three score years and ten with plenty of time for God later—Stop and think! The wages of sin are still misery and death, but mercy, forgiveness, joy, and love still await the prodigals. Come back to Christ. **(Matt 13:1-23, Luke 15:11-32)**

(66) Maybe you started with God and gave up because tragedy, the world, or youthful or sexual pleasures lured you; you put your ambitions first, or maybe sin weighs you down. God loves you, and nothing can separate you from His love. He'll remain faithful even if you live out of His blessing, for the covenant you made with Him is binding, and that's despite yourself. It's never too late or too soon to return to God. **(Luke 15:11-31, 1 John 1:5-9)**

(67) Don't confuse demons with the flesh, the world, and sin. Sloth, laziness, disobedience, pride, anger, unforgivingness, self-pity, ignorance, and lack of belief aren't always the tunes of the devil. Attitude change and repentance are regularly required to level up your life. If you're backslidden, you're wasting Christ's call to help and bless others, and especially yourself; you are missing out on your true vocation, lasting joy, and peace.
(Matt 28:16-19, Gal 5:7, Heb 12:1)

(68) When the cock crows: The disciple Peter failed a lot, and on one occasion spectacularly, but Christ never abandoned him. God wanted to change and improve Peter through his character faults. It's tough to get rid of what we think we are and then replace it with what God wants us to be. You may have stepped out of your boat and sunk before, but growth means facing your mistakes, hang-ups, anxieties, and fears. Push the boat out, and do some more water-walking. God's hand will always save.
(Matt 14:22-32, John 21:15-17)

(69) *'Call and I will rescue.'* We don't have a fickle God, a busy Jesus, or a part time Holy Spirit. They're full on full time; their love limitless, especially when we fail. The prodigal son made a huge mistake, spent his inheritance, and found the world's gutter before returning home. He feared what his father might say, but he was welcomed, forgiven, and restored. Call out—God's listening. No problem or sin too big for Him. **(Ps 34, Luke 15:11-32)**

(70) Need a fresh start in life? Maybe you call yourself 'Christian' but have no concept of a life with Him who created you. Maybe you have lost your first love, Christ. Unlike New Year resolutions, God's love and forgiveness are not fleeting, and they will never abandon you. Whose comforts will you seek today? Will it be the world's which are fragile and fleeting, your own flesh which is fickle and unreliable (to say the least), or will you call to the one who created you for greater things? **(Ps 70:4, Luke 15:11-32, Rev 2:4)**

(71) Sin entices with promises of fun, but it's candy-coated poison; sin is packed with haunting consequences, fat with hurt, sickness, regret, and spiritual death. Then there's the host of demons inherited from playing the devil's subtle games, believing his lies; controlling spirits bent on your misery and destruction. Christ came to clean your slate, to give you a new life. His Holy Spirit can renew your mind and set you on the right course. Put matters right with God today and move on. **(1 John 1:9, Rev 3:20)**

(72) If you think no one cares or loves you, well, Christ does and He's prepared to love you unconditionally and watch over you forever. That's despite whatever you've done in the past, which, amazingly, God chooses never to recall. *'He removes your sin as far as the east is from the west.'* The Father loves you unconditionally. Check His word . . . nowhere does it say that those who call on His name will be ignored, shunned, punished, stay sick or full of demons and fears, be condemned, or live without forgiveness, hope, and renewal. Accept Christ and let the Holy Spirit have all of you!
(Ps 103:12, 1 John 1:19)

Barrie Kibble

MINDSET
'Life cannot be conquered until you've conquered yourself.'

(73) GOOD NEWS: It's entirely up to *you* what you think about today; it doesn't have to be fear, dread, misery, worry, or what the devil normally offloads on you. Your mind isn't controlled by the devil, your circumstances, or other people unless you want it to be. *'Take every thought captive and make it obedient to Christ.'* The power to choose what you think lies in your hands. Maybe it's time you made a stand and changed your thought life.
(Rom 12:2, 2 Cor 10:5)

(74) If you're not going to think positively today then no one else can do it for you. You can't rely on other people's faith, strength, love, gift, or calling to replace or supplement yours. God has called you as you are with all your faults and assets, and although He fills you with the Holy Spirit, you've got to *'work out your own salvation with awe and trembling.'* So what facet of your life are you going to work on with God today? **(Phil 2:12)**

(75) Is anything too difficult for God? No, but what He can do is often hamstrung by our lack of active faith (we know He can, but we're not sure He will). What we continually think and say about a situation is critically important. If we speak God's word according to His will about anything, Christ says nothing is impossible to us. Step out in faith for someone or something today and see it already answered in your minds eye. *'Call into being that which does not exist as if it did exist.'* **(Jer 32:27, Rom 4:17)**

(76) Replace worry at the centre of your life with Christ. What we let into our minds is entirely up to us; whatever we meditate on will take root in our hearts and its fruit shall come out of our mouths. *'Be anxious for nothing, but in everything by prayer and supplication with thanksgiving tell God about your every concern. His peace will guard your heart and mind.'* Fill up with His word and live in obedience according to His investment in Christ in you. The peace of God is beyond all riches, so let's face the music and dance. **(Matt 6:25-34, Phil 4:6-7)**

(77) Fear paralyses us, turning our lives to misery; it keeps us from stepping out in God's will and grasping life to the full. Fear that produces a calm caution is natural, but irrational fear cripples us. Renewing the mind is key, accomplished by continually applying God's word to our fears. *'God hasn't given you a spirit of fear, but of power, love, and a sound mind.'* You need to confront your fears—go tell the past and the devil exactly what God says, and start to live free of debilitating fear. **(2 Tim 1:7** *AMP***)**

(78) Your thought life affects everything you do. For your own confidence, peace, and joy you need to change the negative about yourself, situations, and people—even before you get up in the morning. The Holy Spirit will help renew your mind, but He requires both your agreement and your assistance. *'God will keep in perfect peace whose mind is stayed on Him.'*
(Isa 26:3, Rom 8:5-6, 12:2, Eph 4:22-24)

(79) Christ didn't go around asking for money, preaching self, or boasting how great His ministry was. He lived by pure faith, compassion and humility, and showed us how the kingdom worked. He never refused a broken and contrite heart. He sat with sinners. He came to bring people back to the Father of mankind to show life wasn't by chance. He came to heal and deliver people. He didn't come to build separate denominations, but the one true church. He left us with the Holy Spirit—the power that created everything. Why not think about what Christ means to you today?
(Luke 19:10, John 10:25-30, Acts 1:1-10)

(80) Are you tired, angry, tearful, fed up, maybe you doubt God's existence? The devil skulks about the corners of your mind looking for an open window or door. What triggered your sudden malaise? Were you hurt, haunted by the past, sickness, that habitual sin you thought you had a handle on, sadness, fear or dread, or you realize you still haven't truly forgiven someone? The list could be endless, but God's grace isn't. Go talk to Him. The devil seeks to steal your joy, destroy your peace, and sever you from God. Recognise your true enemy and guard your thought-life. Don't rely on your own reasoning—obey the leading of the Holy Spirit.
(John 10:10, Rom 6:16, 2 Tim 1:14)

(81) A mind set on earthly pursuits has little time for God. No worldly desire can protect our souls or give us permanent peace. We work out our salvation as we stick close to God; set our hearts and minds on His designs and promises. Relationships grow from time spent together; they grow stronger with each meeting. Time spent with God is never wasted. Do so with expectant joy, not from a sense of duty or religious observance. God is our father, not some ancient white-haired caricature invented for Christmas. He is all yours, alive and upfront. And you are all His!
(Exod 34:14, Ps 42:1, 62:8, 84:2, Matt 5:8)

(82) Reasoning: Trust to God in decision-making not human reasoning. Rely on His word rather than your own perception of situations. Keep your mind set on what God wants and not what rusts or collects dust. Place others needs first and yours second. The past will try to colour and determine your future: let it go—let God do a new thing. Thoughts are like sheep: let them wander and they get themselves into all sorts of peril and difficulties. Keep your mind fixed on God, and He will come through for you.
(Isa 43:19, 55:8, Matt 6:19-20)

(83) We are a house of thoughts. We try hard to keep burglars out of our secular property, but then we go and leave a window unlocked in our spirituality. The flesh invades, and we give into any old thought and make it our own. Our lusts and needs run our every moment, or demons break in to thieve or destroy everything we hold dear. They daub our walls with graffiti: Fear, gossip, pride, jealousy, anger, unforgivingness, and rebellion. The wrong thoughts can steal our peace, ransack our joy and hope, hurt others, and leave us in chaos. Learn to *'Take every thought captive for Christ.'* **(2 Cor 10:5)**

(84) Life's defeats or victories occur on the battlefields of our mind. Our chosen thought patterns will either bless us or cause misery and chaos. Thoughts birth words and actions, and we live to regret our wrong choices. Thoughts rule attitude and habit. We best think hard about what we think, for our thoughts form the words and actions that govern and steer our lives. Who will you give control of your mind to today? There's no middle ground—it's a fight to the spiritual death. Renew and strengthen your mind with Bible verses, positive thoughts, and dwell on the goodness, faithfulness, and promises of God despite what the world, the flesh, and the devil throw at you today. **(Rom 6:19-21, Gal 5:22-24, Titus 2:12)**

(85) What's worse than being in two minds? Remaining there! Trying to walk in two directions at once takes us nowhere. We expend precious energy for nothing, neither doing nor being, cold nor hot, but inactive, helpless to ourselves and others—impotent, barren. Whatever we do, we mustn't stay there; it's the most miserable, soul-destroying place on earth. Don't stagnate in worry, indecision and procrastination. Isolate the problem; seek sound council. Pray about the issue; break it down into manageable proportions; make a decision and take a firm step of faith. Then leave everything with God. **(Prov 13:10, James 1:5-8)**

(86) Have you lost your peace? The battle for your soul is through your mind. *'Take every thought captive and make it obedient to Christ', 'God will keep in perfect peace whose mind is stayed on Him.'* PEACE equals trust, joy, well-being, confidence, and hope. Living out *the word* takes practice and perseverance, but it gets easier. Make sure you're walking right with God and under his blessing by confessing, and then reading, believing, and speaking His word. Nothing else changes you, or any situation, or anyone else. Get your peace back. **(Isa 26:3, Phil 4:6-7)**

(87) Let Christ replace worry at the centre of your life with Himself. What we let into our minds is entirely up to us; whatever we meditate on will take root in our hearts and its fruit shall come out of our mouths. *'Be anxious for nothing, but in everything by prayer and supplication with thanksgiving tell God about your every concern. His peace will guard your heart and mind.'* Fill up with His word, and live in obedience according to His investment in Christ in you. **(Phil 4:6-7)**

(88) Worry is simply refusing to trust God with our problems. It's not arrogant or foolhardy to say, "I'm not going to be anxious about anything today." That's a bold statement fat with faith which pleases God. Jesus said, *'Don't worry,'* so we can lay EVERY problem at his feet. But we have to let go of the problems. It takes practice to act on God's word. We have to get into His word, learn verses by heart, and apply them to our mind when needed. **(2 Tim 2:15** *AMP***)**

Barrie Kibble

PRAYER

'You'll see more from your knees than standing tiptoe atop
wishful thinking.'

(89) Christ died and was resurrected chiefly to make a way back to God for us. The Father tore the thick, temple curtain in two supernaturally. We can now enter directly into God's presence. No need for a scapegoat as sacrifice for sin, or a high priest to accept it. The price paid once and for all. God says, "Step directly into My presence for I see you as righteous through My Son." His grace is precious, don't stifle it, stamp on it, ignore or reject it—live in grace and enjoy it. **(Matt 27:51, Heb 10:19-20, Rev 5:9-11)**

(90) *'If God is for us who can be against us?'* Look away from self; take your eyes and thoughts off situations and people who cause you problems and focus on what God thinks about you, because it's all good! He has no problem accepting you as you are. He knows you from the day you were born to the day He takes you home, and He knows what is best for your life and contentment. Learn from the prophets—get off your high horse and get on your knees, and you'll experience the power of God in your life. **(Rom 8:1-17, 31** *AMP***)**

(**91**) We need God's help all the time. One of the most important and simplest of prayers is, "God, please help me." KISS: *Keep it super simple* is a writing term in fiction. Don't complicate matters with religiosity. Don't get despondent or confused by trying to formulate clever sounding liturgy, just speak in faith. You can use this prayer a thousand times a day and God always answers; it's based on solid biblical principles. All things are possible with God! (**Ps 30:2, 56:9, 109:26, Matt 19:26, Heb 4:16**)

(**92**) There's nothing more intimate and powerful at the altar of prayer than to place the Holy Spirit foremost. Connect to God's power. Ask the Spirit what He wants you to pray before you get your list out. When you use a kettle, you don't just put water in it, wait with faith, and then wonder why it's not boiling—you have to switch it on. Prayer and intercession are never mundane or impotent when you tap into God's power.
(**Ps 141:2, Prov 15:29, Matt 21:22, Rom 12:12, Eph 6:18, Col 4:2, James 5:16**)

(93) Let your words blossom into Godly action, transformed by Godly thoughts and aligned with God's will. Then you'll enjoy peace and joy beyond human understanding. What is God's will? It's His word. His word is Christ made flesh, Christ personified, Christ in action through prayer. Prayer is not simply words lost to air. When we pray the will of God using His word, His divine power radically changes people and situations, just as God sent out his word in the beginning and formed the universe. Today, choose God inspired words—*'the fervent prayer of the righteous'* gets the job done. **(John 1:1-5, James 5:16)**

(94) Don't give up on your prayers because they're not being answered. Stand firm, for persistent faith will carry you through every battle to victory. Stop believing your enemies are flesh and blood—they're spiritual! Testing and stretching puts iron into your faith. Spiritual fights aren't won with your fists, but on your knees. Despite 13 years in an Egyptian prison, Joseph kept hold of his vision because he trusted God's perfect timing, not his own intellect. *'God's ways are not our ways, nor are His thoughts our thoughts.'* Never give up. Make a stand on your knees! **(Exod 14:13, Isa 55:8, Luke 21:9, 1 Cor 16:13, Eph 6:12-16)**

(95) Prevailing prayer is the mark of a Christian who means business with God. Praying people take time to get alone with God and talk to Him like a close friend, no airs and graces, just penitent hearts full of worship with a vision underscored by faith and hope; a vision that burns brightly despite all that the devil, the flesh, and the world can muster against them. They trust God wholly. They believe in His power completely. *'No weapon formed against you shall prosper.'* The prayer of such men and women overcomes all and gets the right answers. **(Isa 54:17, Acts 12:5, James 5:16)**

(96) If you're frustrated that those you witness to are not saved, especially family and friends, you need to know the key: patient, persistent, faith-filled prayer—first and last! Dead works and doubt result otherwise. *'You must bind the strong man to plunder his house.'* For the gospel is absolute foolishness to those whose eyes and ears are shut by the devil. Consistent and persistent prayer in the word of God pries the lost from the kingdom of darkness and brings freedom to its captives.
(Mark 3:27, Rom 5:3-4, 1 Cor 1:18, James 1:3)

(97) The devil takes the negative events that befall us and loves to remind us of them. We often nurture those bad experiences with self-pity or unforgivingness, or use them as a crutch to explain our attitudes, problems and failures, or we simply blame God. God isn't ignorant of the bad things that happen, but we hamstring His ability to act through our lack of prayer. Prayer opens the doors to the warehouses of heaven. He warns us through prayer of impending disaster so we can be ready for it, then go though it or maybe avoid it altogether. Don't stagnate; you have to accept and then let go of the past to be able to fully embrace the future.
(Ps 139:23, Isa 33:17-19, Matt 6:9-13)

(98) If you're serious about hearing from God, you have to get on your knees and stay there until you wrestle out His will for you. Why wrestle like Jacob? Because then you'll be assured of God's direction, and you'll never forget that moment or what He said despite what people and the devil throw at you. Avoid pain, heartbreak, and needless trouble—take everything to God in prayer.
(Gen 32:24-26, Phil 4:6-7)

(99) Often, it's not the giant calamities that pull us down in the end, but the small, seemingly insignificant yet endless attacks on body, soul, spirit, and mind that gradually eat away our peace, joy, health, and happiness; these assaults dull every precious hope and dream. The monster of unbridled stress feeds on that which we overlook or put off for another day; this insatiable beast loves to grow fat on our failures, unforgivingness, worry, hate and anger—all are soul killers. Keep short and accurate accounts with God. **(Matt 11:30, 1 John 1:9)**

(100) Faith is to take God's word literally and act on it. *'Call into being the things that don't exist as if they did.'* Our heads are full of modern thinking, and we question everything; we expect whatever we want to come to us on a plate—we deserve them, it's our right! If we can't see it, it's not real. The Roman Centurion believed in Jesus without question, His lordship, and what He could do, and thus received his servant's healing. Jesus said, *'Pray whatever is in the will of God and you will have it—simply believe.'* This keeps us safe and others blessed, saved, comforted, restored, healed, and open to change. **(Luke 7:1-10)**

(101) We worry and stress about many things, often keeping them to ourselves, determining to fight through all the hopelessness, misery, and despair. God wants ALL of your concerns and anxieties even if you brought them upon yourself. He delights to undertake for His beloved. *'The battle is the Lord's',* not yours. *'Cast ALL your cares upon Him.'* Fear, arrogance, foolishness, and pride grasp onto worry and suffering. Why stifle divine help? *'Trust in Him with all your heart, mind, and soul and never lean on your own understanding,'* and remember: *'There is no condemnation for those in Christ.'* Who you are is forever settled in heaven. What you do is worked out on earth.
(Prov 3:5-6, Rom 8:1, 1 Peter 5:7)

(102) When you pray God's will, you need to be ready to see God answer that prayer as *He chooses*. Often we see the situation worsen, and we wonder if He's taking us seriously, or even heard our pleas at all. The truth is: The devil fires his worse broadside just before his ammunition runs out—suddenly our answer to prayer is seen just as the dust settles! We pray and the devil reacts, but God always fires the last shot. Keep praying with faith, led and guided by the Holy Spirit. **(Ps 55:18, Jer 20:13, Dan 6:27, Rom 8:14, 2 Cor 4:18)**

(103) Search for God in the small things, the little miracles of daily life. A person saved, someone healed, answers to prayer, mountains moved, love perfected, forgiveness, mercy, restoration, and the return of prodigal sons and daughters from the wilderness. All flow out of the big thing: a prayer relationship with the Father of life, the embodiment of love. The big thing is simply the divine seal on every small thing. **(Gen 49:25-26, Deut 28:2, Isa 12:3, Zech 4:10, Eph 1:3)**

(104) The storehouses of God are overflowing, and everything in them is freely available to His children at their time of need. If we can't see this abundance with faith's eye, it won't be realised. Timing is all to do with listening. We learn about faith and how to apply it. Faith and patience go hand in hand. Best make sure our relationship with Him is right first, for although His love is unfaltering and steadfast, we can delay, waste, or cut off our blessings. **(Deut 28:12, Hab 2:3, Mark 11:24, John 15:7, 2 Cor 1:20)**

(105) To change anything by prayer, we need to stay with it until the flesh is conquered and faith is perceived. *'The constant, fervent prayer of a righteous person accomplishes much.'* This is aggressive, overcoming, fruit-filled faith.
(Matt 11:12, Phil 4:6-7, Heb 5:7, James 5:16)

(106) *'Nothing is impossible with God.'* Are you for Him, heart, mind, and soul? Then every blessing is yours in the heavenly realms. That doesn't mean everything you want is yours—it means everything you need is yours. Ask and simply believe.
(Matt 17:20, Luke 1:37, 18:27, Heb 11:6)

(107) Abiding with God: Knowing His will, and with a simple faith empowered by the Holy Spirit, you can do what Jesus did and greater things! Your passion-full prayers can change the bad to good, despair to hope, the lost to Christ, dark into light, and the impossible to the possible. Prayer is an intrinsic part of your Christ-like nature, like the vital oil required for a machine to run efficiently. **(Ps 91, John 4:12)**

(108) Enthusiastic Prayer: When we believe in something and enjoy practicing it, we put all our effort, strength, and talent into it. We can do the same with prayer, *if* we long for answers: prayer for every situation and person under the sun. Lost your passion? Look to the examples of Jesus and find a fresh perspective. Every prayer He fashioned was answered, most of them immediate and miraculous! You need to ask yourself why prayer worked for Him. **(Col 3:23)**

(109) Fickle Feelings: Don't base your attitude to prayer on feelings. They're unreliable, fleeting, twisting our perceptions of self, people, church, and God. Feelings complicate our decision making and reactions. Feelings are like ships—one minute the sea of life is dead calm and the next it's throwing you about in a storm. Pray from the heart and soul in truth; base your prayer on unalterable fact and the imperishable word of God, not your feelings. **(Matt 26:41, John 3:6, Rom 8:5-13, Eph 6:12)**

(110) Faith and patience go hand in hand. Tarry a while as the promises mature. Wait patiently for the Lord. *'Christ is the word made flesh.'* Hold fast to His word. *'Ask anything in His name and you shall receive.'* *'Trust in Him and the Father shall supply all your needs according to His glorious riches in Christ Jesus.'* God loves to hear your prayers and answer them, but He longs more to simply fellowship with you. **(Isa 40:31, John 14:14, Phil 4:19)**

(111) Simply Believe: We grow up forgetting that as children we trusted totally in our parents' provision, our every need met with cast-iron sureties. They fulfilled their promises at birthdays and Christmas' to give us our desires; at other times they wisely kept from us things we thought we needed but would've harmed us. We never doubted their promises or wisdom. Why doubt God, the parent of the impossible? **(Mark 9:23, John 16:26 -28, Gal 4:6)**

(112) Faith-fuelled prayer calls into being what is promised but not seen. It isn't a case of will God answer, but the assurance that He does answer. Having an overcoming prayer life is talking about the promise not the problem, the plaster not the cut. Keep staring at the mountain and it gets bigger, but keep looking at God and the mountain shrinks; sometimes it simply vanishes! Infuse and empower your prayer life with faith. **(Heb 11:1-39, Matt 6:5-14)**

(113) Never Give Up: Pray God's will and answers will come. *'His words never return to Him empty.'* We'll never fully understand God's timing, but it's perfect. In our fast-food society, we expect the instant. Link overcoming faith with prayer and add resoluteness to your armoury. God still does the instant, yet the measure and timing of an answer is often according to the belief, motive, and intention of our hearts interlocking with God's plan.
(Isa 55:11, Hosea 6:3, Matt 7:9-11, Gal 6:9, Phil 3:12, Heb 12:1-3)

(114) Blockages: Sin blocks blessings and answer to prayer—repent and then tackle the issues. Maybe someone's spiritual life or salvation depends on your forgiveness. Often we need to change a negative thought pattern or attitude. Get rid of every hindrance so that we can enter God's presence with expectation and praise. Paul found prayer involves a clean slate, humility, thanksgiving, and agreeing with God's will. **(Rom 6:23, Gal 3:1-3)**

(115) Faith is integral to prayer. It's not faith in self or the prayer, but faith that God will answer. *'If you lack faith then ask God for more.'* Breakthrough in prayer often follows a fervent period of knee-business. It isn't that God doesn't hear us, but we battle with dark spiritual forces as well as our own flesh. God stretches us through patience and practice, and we become bolder in prayer. Press through. **(Mark 9:24, Rom 10:17, 2 Pet 3:15)**

(116) '*Without faith it is impossible to please God.*' If you need more faith, then ask Him. '*He will withhold no good thing from those He loves.*' Prayer without faith is like riding a bike without wheels—you get nowhere fast. Find out what God's word says about any given situation and then pray with the wealth of faith that rises within you. **(Ps 84:11, Eph 3:12, Heb 10:23, 11:6)**

(117) Prayer has to be in line with the word of God. The word of God is the will of God; it's potent; powerful beyond human understanding. Pray His word and mountains are moved, situations change, and people are saved. Forget the stock 'Seven Steps' to everything and find a way to pray that works for you guided by the Holy Spirit. Relish those times. Abide with God and His word, and you'll always pray His will. **(Ezra 8:23, Prov 3:3, Col 1:9)**

Barrie Kibble

REPENTANCE

'Saying sorry isn't as costly as saying nothing.'

(118) Surrender all: The way to peace and contentment in all situations is to stay surrendered to God. Let the Holy Spirit continually renew your mind. Confess your doubt, pride, fear, spirit of dead religion, and fleshy works. Realise that you can't do this Christian stuff on your own—and you don't have to! With God, victory starts with surrender.
(Deut 20:4, 2 Sam 8:14, Ps 20:6, 44:6-7, 1 John 5:4)

(119) Christians who persist in sin might get by with lip-service to God and a hearty sing song on a Sunday but little else. God promises to never abandon us, but we can't expect Him to bless, answer prayer, or move us forward if we court sin. There's no power in the Christian walk if we knowingly grieve the Holy Spirit and could care less. God will always forgive our transgressions if we repent. Earthly hell and misery is us trying to find Christ while worshiping the devil. Show me a discontented Christian with many woes and I'll show you a Bible that gathers dust, knees that never bend, and a haughty spirit poisoned with sin. **(Eph 4:30, 1 John 1:9)**

(120) Departing from evil and sin brings health to flesh and strength to bones, as well as peace, joy, and contentment in every situation, in every tribulation. Taste and see that God is true to His every word. Misery is a heart weighed down with sin –joy is a heart uncluttered by the flesh, the past, and the world's ways. Get on your knees before you fall flat on your face. Your God is full of love, compassion, and grace, and is quick to forgive and forget. *'Come unto me all you who are heavy laden and I will give you rest.'* **(Ps 34:8, Prov 3:8, Matt 11:30)**

(121) Like a virus, sin permeates and poisons everything we do, and hope to achieve; it delays God's blessings. Joshua had to sort out a soldier who went against God's commands. The army had been victorious at every turn but was suddenly defeated because of this man's sin. If you continue in your sin, it renders you ineffective in every area of your life. The Holy Spirit is rendered inactive in us by any trace or vestige of sin. Repentance sets us free, restores our peace, and releases us into God's promises again. **(Josh 7, 1 John 1:9)**

(122) If you play with fire you get burnt. Temptation is a natural enemy, but giving into what we know is bad for body and mind damages our spirit and soul, deadens the heart, and corrupts our relationship with God. God tempts no person, but He allows temptation so you can conquer it through Christ and grow. Your blessings and peace of mind depend on confession. We damage ourselves and halt kingdom-living if we covet sin. Repent and find restoration in the God of second chances.
(Matt 4:1, 1 Cor 10:13, 1 Thess 3:5, Heb 2:18, 4:15, James 1:14)

(123) Ours is the gospel of the second chance: Peter betrayed Christ three times, Paul hounded Christians; King David killed a woman's husband so he could have her. The Bible is full of imperfect people God could use to change the world because they were broken and remade through repentance. Repent. Pick yourself up, dust yourself off, deal with the consequences, and move on. Let's face the music and dance. **(Ps 130:4, Eph 1:7, Heb 12:5)**

(124) Thanks to Christ, we can break the cycle of sin. We make it a habit to repent and God forgives us, restores us, and releases his blessings over and over again, but growing in grace also hinges on forgiving those who've hurt or damaged us. While it's wonderful to have God forgive us completely and never bring our mistakes to mind, it doesn't negate us from saying sorry and making peace with those we have hurt by our words and actions both now and in the past. **(Job 22:21, Mark 9:50, Heb 12:11, 2 Pet 3:14)**

(125) What better time to get right with God than right now. Let Him show you it's good on His side of the fence; that you don't need what you're desperately grasping onto; what's harming your body, mind and spirit, even though you thought it safe to hide in it. God only wants you free to fulfil your potential with peace and joy, not just remove what you believe is your last grip on a world, which, if you were honest uses you, and doesn't want or like you anyway. The devil ensures that, so best get right with God. **(Matt 16:26, John 12:46, 15:18)**

(126) For many selfish or fearful reasons we're quick to write people off when they fail us or don't measure up to our beliefs, goals, and standards. God writes no one off—ever—and is displeased when we so easily condemn and abandon others by using His word to reinforce our own weighing scales, plans, mindsets, and inadequacies. Unconditional love can conquer all and must start with self, but un-confessed pride, self-ambition, and hidden fears, imprison every selfish soul to the detriment of all. Be careful how you use the label 'Christian' if you can't be measured by it. Best get that plank out of your eye first. **(Jer 33:3, Matt 7:3-5, Eph 1:1-23)**

(127) Sin contaminates all our hopes and dreams, and it brings fresh enmity between us and God; we render God's work in us inactive and His blessings dry up. Sin breaks the back of peace. Putting sin right is far better for mind, soul, and body than struggling to hide and hold onto it. If you carried double your own bodyweight around on your back every day but didn't have too, how miserable is that! So why carry your sin when Christ died to expunge it? Repentance brings freedom. Go talk to God. **(Isa 61:1, Gal 5:1, 13, 1 Pet 2:16, 19)**

(128) Sin reaps the whirlwind. God doesn't punish anymore as Christ paid for all our sins on the cross. Since then, we store up and bring judgement on ourselves. Sin heaps on us the wages of fear, sickness, misery, and early death. Realise sooner than later that you *will* get a return from whatever you have invested in, good or bad, and in full measure with interest! God is patient and His grace awaits those who repent and seek Him. Best talk to God today and put matters right.
(Ps 1:5, Matt 12:36, Rom 14:10, 2 Cor 5:10, 1 Tim 5:24, 1 John 4:17)

(129) We can't continue in sin and think we're immune to its debilitating affects. Christ died once for all, He can't die again. God's grace isn't a get-out-of-jail-card. If we continue in deliberate sin we become meat for the devil. He'll tear us apart with guilt, fear, sickness and oppression. *'The last state of that person will be worse than the first.' 'Do we sin more so that grace will abound? Heaven forbid for that makes a trifle of the cross.'* Put things right with God today and you'll start to live in peace, grow again, and receive His favour. **(Matt 12:43-45, Rom 6:1-3)**

(130) Don't let past failures haunt you. God's bigger than them. There's ample room at the cross for your mistakes, horrendous moments, terrible decisions, lies, rejection, false-witness, bad judgements, gossip and sin. *'Look, can you not see God is doing a new thing?'* Why let the past control your today or your future? Get your mind out of the trash—confess all, for He forgives all. Grasp a fresh perspective of God's grace and move on with His blessing. **(Isa 42:9, 43:19)**

(131) The Psalms tell us a lot about King David's heart. How we deal with our sin tells us a lot about ourselves. God isn't fooled, as He knows the thoughts of our hearts. David had a heart after God, quick to recognise his sin and repent, and God was quick to restore him. David grew stronger and wiser. Praise, peace, and fresh growth are a result of those battles. The devil wants you down and out because of your bad habits, faults, and weaknesses—God wants you back up and fruitful, and how quickly that happens is up to you. **(Ps 51:10, Matt 5:8, Acts 13:22, 1 Tim 1:5)**

(132) Rebellion or obedience: There's nothing more debilitating to our happiness and contentment than guilt. If we want to get rid of every last scrap of nagging or overwhelming guilt we need to get right with God by confessing our sin. God is ever faithful and just to forgive the repentant heart, restore the damaged soul, and cleanse us from all unrighteousness! Maintain a healthy conscience and protect your peace by keeping a clear slate with your Heavenly Father. **(Ps 25:11, Matt 12:37, Acts 15:10** *AMP*, **1 John 1:9)**

Barrie Kibble

.

DIRECTION
'A map is a boon if you can read it.'

(133) Like Jackie Pullinger, Gladys Aylward, Burton, and countless others, when God gives you a vision you'll often have to go against religious people, church convention, and sometimes friends and family to pursue it. Never fear, what God gives you, He also anoints you to do, and He instils the ability to do it. Live by faith for every need and don't shrink back, or you'll live in regret for the rest of your life. **(Heb 11)**

(134) What's your calling? Seek wise council yes, but ignore the naysayers and doom-mongers. Listen only for God speaking to your heart and spirit through His word for confirmation to step out. The Holy Spirit will help you fulfil your God-given ministry against all odds. God will anoint, equip, bless, and strengthen you; supply your every need. Be courageous like Joshua, and don't be afraid to do what you were born to do. **(Josh 1)**

(135) Rome wasn't built in a day, so don't rush ahead of God. If you can't face people, you can face God because what He cares about is His relationship with you, and it's not meant for others to govern, fathom, or imagine. Seek wise advice and council, but only ever move on what God says to your spirit. If He doesn't speak immediately, you've got to wait until He does speak. That's awfully tough sometimes—and boy I know!—but it's the right and only way into future blessings.
(Ps 37:7, 40:1, Eccles 3:1-9, Isa 40:31, Rom 8:25, James 5:7)

(136) When God lays out your future, He doesn't dwell on your past. People do, but their thoughts and plans are foolishness to God, for nothing can thwart His will. Be ever so courageous and keep moving forward; take no thought for what has been. God uses everything to suit His purposes for you. Nothing is wasted in shaping you for heaven. God has fashioned certain doors that can only be opened by you. Start opening doors today, for faith without action is like trying to fill a sieve with water.
(Phil 3:7-9, 14, James 2:14-26)

(137) If you're anxious or confused about the direction of your life or what God wants to say to you, you've probably isolated yourself from Him, or the devil's engineered the gap. The way to break free, to receive clarity and revelation is to, *'Lean your entire personality on God and His word.'* Trust Him without reservation. Take the risky leap of faith and dare to believe your every move and breath is safe in His hands. I lean on Him everyday, and it's the only way I know how to survive. Believe me, like you, I have tried everything else and . . . nothing else works! **(Prov 3:5)**

(138) God can use unlikely people and situations to get our attention. Want to walk with God? Then get in step with Him. Stop the narrow thinking, relying on old works, rushing ahead, bowing to fear or acting on emotion and feelings. Check everything with God. Often, He asks you to go a different way, leaving people bemused or upset—trust them to God. Be obedient and blessed. God's will done in your life is all that matters when you meet Him face-to-face. **(Phil 2:12)**

(139) There are times when we force ourselves down avenues and take on jobs and projects that are nothing to do with what God wants for our healthy growth. We struggle on frustrated, lifeless, and bored; we curse others and aren't happy with ourselves. Be careful where you walk if you haven't talked to God about every step and waited patiently for His answer. When you do step out in His name you'll know—the right doors will open and the blessings will flow. **(Ps 27:14, 37:23)**

(140) *'God knows the end from the beginning.'* All we need to do is lean on Him, rely on Him, and trust in Him. He knows what's going to unfold. He knows how much trouble you can handle to put iron in your faith and grace in your prayers, and He knows the exact time to turn on the blessings. If this is the God we worship, then we've nothing to worry about as long as we keep our eyes on Christ, our feet firmly on *The Narrow Way*. **(Isa 46:10, Matt 16:24, Rev 21:6)**

(141) Stuck in a rut? Seek God and find out what He wants you to do; turn your feet in the direction He wants you to go. Start walking and you'll get there. Apply hope and faith to Kingdom matters. You must overcome your practice of fear, your old habits of belief in anything but God's precepts and will. If you're not growing and overcoming, you're stationary and ineffective. God will expand your borders and increase you if you *'simply believe'* and step out with unwavering faith. **(Ps 9:10, 34:10, Prov 8:17, Jer 33:3, Matt 6:33)**

(142) Seek wise council. Many give advice to suit their own ends or to impose their will on you. Some will simply side with you because they like you, while others will give ill-advice because they don't like your friends, your beliefs, views and passions—or indeed you! Some give unsound and ungrounded spur-of-the-moment advice, while others use guesswork or are motivated by emotion. The right people put you first; they listen, guide, and encourage, speak from sound knowledge and experience, and always point to the cross. **(Prov 1:5, 11:14, 24:6, John 14:26, 1 Cor 12:28)**

(143) *'Surely goodness and mercy shall follow me all my life.'*
Stick close to God and you'll be fine. There are over 365 promises
in your Bible-bank. Learn them, live in them, speak them, and think
them. You can use them like a cheque book; cash them in when you
need them most. That sort of faith and trust comes from walking
close to God; knowing His will for you at every step. Sheep listen
carefully to every command of a good shepherd, because they
know he knows what's best for them. **(Ps 23:6, John 10:14, 2 Cor 1:20)**

(144) '*Paths of righteousness for His sake.*' Better to walk the
beaten paths of God's word than risk the untried tracks of the
world's short cuts to spirituality. Shifting shale, loose rock, sheer
drops, and no signposts lead you into danger, sin, and false piety
not God's glory reflected in you. Many will mock you, but self-
gain, self-deceit, and falsehood is their map. The good shepherd
leads his sheep on safe paths for their ultimate blessing.
(Ps 23, John 14:6)

(145) Sometimes God asks you to do the ridiculous before He'll do the miraculous. Hearing His words of direction is paramount, but just as important is 'the stepping out'. He lets you take the first step in faith, just as Peter did on water and Moses before pharaoh. That's how we learn and grow in our faith. Then, when we're under pressure, we can look back and recall the faithfulness of our heavenly Father. **(Ps 91:4, Lam 3:22-24, 1 Cor 1:18)**

CHANGE

'The most rewarding of journeys is into yourself.'

(146) Like it or not, life's a free-running rollercoaster, and it's the same for everyone, rich or poor, good or bad. Straight runs, tunnels, peaks and troughs, slow and fast bits, dangerous bends, sudden changes in direction—especially reverse—most times going nowhere fast. Tears and laughter, fear and joy; people step on and off, some good some bad, some wonderful and some downright evil. Few are keepers. Rain, sun, fog and ice, breakdowns and hold-ups, accidents and time in the repair shop. Yet it all means absolutely nothing, it's all wasted unless you know where you're headed. Make sure God's at the wheel and holding the map. Thankfully, He knows the big WHY of it all, *and* your ultimate destination! **(Prov 3:5-6, John 10:10)**

(147) Keep your heart pure. Consider what you ask for and whether it lines up with God's will—not fleshy desires or wishful thinking—you'll find what you want and what you need are vastly different. Seek wise council before you make a major change in your life. Trust to God and not to your moods, feelings, attitudes or fears. Kingdom living is not about worldly happiness, or fleshy pursuits, but about the needs of others, love, joy, peace, sacrifice, obedience, and worship. **(Ps 51:10, Matt 5:8, Heb 10:22)**

(148) Spiritual railway stations 1: A busy junction often brings frustration, confusion, and panic. Hectic decisions are all demanded at once as we change trains, our contentment and comfort temporarily sacrificed. The reliable clickity-clack of wheels against steel is replaced by an array of destinations, an indistinguishable racket of voices. Until we locate our next train and settle into our new seat, we need to stay focused on the ultimate destination. Change moves us onward to places that need to be reached, and they in turn, like an invisible force, want us to reach them. God knows the why of it. Trust Him. **(Phil 4:6-7)**

(149) Spiritual railway stations 2: Life's journey is often interrupted when a train breaks down. We're confronted with the unknown and its wearisome baggage of insecurity. Stranded in an empty waiting room, we flip through tattered magazines that speak of past glories and the safety of old applause. Envious of the frequent trains that stop on the down-track platform, we are sorely tempted to cross the bridge and join the silent crowds going back. But it's precisely then that we must grasp our ticket as if it's life itself, and with hope, patience, and blind faith, set our face for the next up-track train. Trust Him. **(Rom 15:13)**

(150) Do you need to grow? Christianity isn't solely a weekly trip to church or a midweek house group. Neither is it just about tithing, or doing nice things to salve your conscience and receive God's approval. Christianity is a one-on-one relationship with the Father of love at all times. Intimacy with Christ through the Holy Spirit should be life changing, and we're continually changed from glory to glory. Get closer to God today and find out what's holding you back. **(Rom 12:12, Phil 2:1-4)**

(151) Non-believers laugh at the notion of a God, yet they're first on their knees when disaster strikes, and then they talk about prayer as if it were commonplace among them, second nature. Normally, the idea of approaching God simply doesn't fit into their lifestyle until they need Him; it's like having a spare beer in the fridge or a sedative in the cupboard just in case trouble strikes. Sadly, a lot of Christians are like this too! Best check where you're spiritually at today. **(Prov 3:5-6, Gal 2:20)**

(152) Lot's wife looked back and turned into a pillar of salt. If you want to move forward you must stop looking back. Abraham, Moses, Joshua, Paul, and many others had to let go of the old life to fully embrace the God-life. Are you depressed, frustrated, or just in a rut? Perhaps your dreams and hopes are floundering on the hard knocks of life. Are you trying to wade through the waist-high mud of indecision or drowning in self-pity? Maybe it's time to clear that crammed and cobwebbed attic in your mind: Fears, regrets, old relationships, hurtful people, negative thought patterns and unforgivingness. Have a huge bonfire, then dust the ash off your shoes and move forward again.
(1 Kings 19:19-21, Luke 9:62, 17:31-33, Phil 3:13-15)

(153) We can change anything negative in our life if we place Christ at the centre; if we surrender all to Him with no 'ifs' or 'buts'. His Spirit will work with us to put things right, help us overcome bad habits, fear, anxiety, lying, dirty thoughts, gossip, unforgivingness, and anything we are willing to surrender and see changed. The process may be tough at first, but it's better to be set free and to live a full life with Christ.
(John 8:36, Rom 12:2, Gal 5:1, Heb 12:12)

(154) God rarely changes us overnight, so we need to be patient; we need to understand and accept that He knows best when and how to mould and shape His beloved. He forms *'beauty out of ashes,'* and always *'releases the imprisoned soul.'* His change, when it comes, is permanent and for our ultimate good. This is what we hold fast to: We get on with life while He works on us. Hang in there, it'll be worth it.
(Isa 61, Col 1:11, 3:12, Heb 6:12, James 1:2-8)

FREEDOM

'Sweeter to the ear is a songbird on the wing than one locked in a cage.'

(155) Why Baptism? When you gave your life to Christ you were 'crucified' with Him. Then, having received the Holy Spirit you are 'made alive' with Christ. To be immersed in water is to be 'buried' with Christ. You can't separate the three and walk the path of victory in freedom, as there will always be something missing. Don't let fear, pride, or embarrassment stop you from living the Christian life as God intended. **(Rom 6:4, 1 Pet 3:21)**

(156) No room for apathy: Kick-start your faith again, and you'll get back your peace and joy, as well as your reason for living. Blessing and sin don't mix, it's like matter and anti-matter. Repent, dust off your Bible, and renew your hope and vision for a wonderful fulfilled life in Christ. Start to help yourself by helping others through good works driven by faith. **(Prov 13:12, John 14:12, Acts 3:19)**

(157) Are you full of dread and anxiety, do you wish tomorrow would never come? God's love restores damaged souls. Stop agreeing with the devil's lies. Repent, and submit to God, for God alone has the answers to all your deep-seated anguish. Let Him rebuild you in Christ's image; set you free to live the fearless life He pre-planned for you. There's no fear in love, so let God love you without reservation, and be set free from despair. He ALWAYS answers those who cry out to Him, but above all, He longs for a deeper relationship with His beloved. That includes you. **(Deut 31:8, Ps 118:6, Prov 3:25, Isa 41:10, 61, Matt 10:31, 1 John 4:18)**

(158) Are you in the devil's honours list? Has he made you a Lord or Dame of worry? Have you been given the Victoria Cross for anxiety? Have you earned an OBE for fear, unforgivingness, or despair? Maybe you got a CBE for going it alone, pride, intransigence, anger, lust, disbelief, or lack of active faith. Perhaps you've earned his greatest accolade, a Knighthood for compromise and apathy. Submit to God, humble yourself, and let Christ set you free! Send those jaded awards and rusty medals back to the pit of hell from whence they came. **(Isa 61, John 10:10)**

(159) The devil isn't bothered by non-Christians, they're marked in his book for misery on earth and permanent death. They spend their days ignoring God, blaspheming the Holy Spirit; locked in their own lusts and desires, haters of others, unforgiving, self-promoters—many are good people who simply try to live right. *All* are sinners suffering now and for eternity. It takes brokenness and courage to seek the God of forgiveness and love, to have His perfect peace, and to be set free by Christ to truly live; to fulfil the true purpose for life, and then to live forever with Him.
(Ps 34:21, 2 Cor 5:1-20)

(160) God's gift of righteousness has no equal and is the guts of grace. You were made right with God once and for all through the cross. Your sin expunged and remembered no more; sin now on the outside and avoidable, not on the inside anymore. Cleansed, restored, and forgiven. The very best you could ever try to do for God is as filthy rags. Live free in Christ, or the world and the devil will smother the truth and the reality of His grace.
(Gen 15:6, Deut 6:25, Isa 64:6, Rom 3:22, 5:17)

(161) Many believe but they keep God at a distance because of fear. Fear of losing what they have due to insecurity. Fear of what others might think. Fear of the unknown. Fear that they might find the truth out about themselves. Fear that their strength will be turned to weakness. Fear that all they have believed in and strived for in life could be pointless. Fear is a major tool of the devil, and people don't realise this until they draw close to God and are set free to be who He meant them to be. Faith has no room for fear. **(Isa 61, Gal 5:1, Eph 3:12, 2 Cor 3:17)**

(162) God can take even the most messed up life and turn it around. People stuck in mud dig ever deeper pits to try and find their way out. Inevitably, the dirty water seeps in and threatens to drown them. Life becomes a series of endless pits zigzagging through their lives like the trenches of the Somme. God says: *"Stop looking down. Look up, reach up, and grab My outstretched hand. Get your eyes off your self and onto Me and I will save you."* **(Ps 40:2, Matt 11:28)**

(163) Irrational fear restricts a rational life. With God, you have no need to face your fears alone. God's way of dealing with personal fear isn't our way, for He knows us more intimately than we know ourselves. Prayer is the key to all things, including past soul and emotional damage that might haunt us today. Call out, and God will gently lead you through your minefields of fear. Trust Him in the darkest moments to deliver you. He will! What he has eagerly done for millions He can also do for you. **(Ps 32:7, 46:1, 2 Tim 1:7)**

(164) If faith isn't in control, then fear is, in one form or another. Just as light overcomes darkness, faith overcomes fear. Faith is like switching on a light—it dispels the darkness, forces it out, and renders it redundant. What will you let your life be controlled by today, every day: Fear or faith? *'Faith comes by hearing and hearing by God's word.'* *'Draw near to God and He will draw near to you.'* **(Rom 10:17, Heb 10:23)**

(165) If it *is* possible to change something negative about self, relationship, place, or circumstance . . . do it. Some 'things', 'places', or 'people' aren't healthy for us, no matter how much we like and cling onto them, and we usually know it in our gut (spirit). Whatever we accept or accumulate comes at a cost; we have to make room for it and protect it. Travel light and retain your freedom, joy, and peace. Maybe it's time for a spiritual check-up; see what God has to say about unwanted baggage and the damage it does. Why not talk to God? **(Ps 68:19, 2 Cor 6:14)**

(166) You may not believe in demons, but they believe in you. Demons enter through sin, life experience, and family history, but they leave one way: through the blood of Christ, and they HAVE to go IF you want them to. Some torment and imprison, others control behaviour, mindset, and sexuality, or use fear and sickness. It's a spiritual battle, and we need to seek wise council. Be prepared to repent and be delivered—set free! *'Greater is He that is in you than he that is in the world.'*
(Matt 4:24, 8:16, 1 Cor 10:21, James 2:19, 1 John 4:4)

(167) We think what we watch and listen to are harmless. Many scoff at the idea of demons; tarot cards are fun, séances a giggle; no harm in mediums, spiritualists or horoscopes, and silly to think that certain radio and TV programmes could possibly induce lifelong depression, horror and fear. The devil takes no prisoners! He sends demons through unguarded doors to poison spirit and soul, steal peace, torment and destroy lives. Be extremely guarded about what you trust in, seek after, listen to, or watch. **(1 Cor 10:21)**

(168) God was working on the details of your life before you were born! He knows your end from your beginning; each day is mapped out, the laughter and the tears, the setbacks and achievements. God gives us life, and within that span is our purpose and passion. When you suddenly realise life isn't about living just for you, it begins to make sense. There's a valid reason for the cross—live every moment in its shadow. **(Eph 1:1-14)**

(169) A faithful friend should guide, mentor, encourage, offer solace, and make your heart light, make you think; keep you on track. They're honest without hurting you, not pushing their dreams at the cost of yours. Otherwise the label doesn't fit, the clothes become tight, and it's time to cast them off. A friend puts you first and last. True friends through thick and thin are precious gems; cleave to them as Christ cleaves to you. **(1 Cor 15:33)**

(170) If money motivates you, God cannot! The misuse and abuse of money is a Siren waiting to shipwreck you on rocks of debt and misery. Spend within your means. If you can' afford something, don't get credit, but rather save for it. Tithe, pay the bills, purchase what you actually need, and save a little. Some of the Godliest people I have met are rich in spirit not wealth. Money hasn't imprisoned them. God ensures they lack no good thing because their trust is in Him and not silver or gold. Remember, the more material stuff you have, the more you must protect.
(Mal 3:8-10, Matt 6:24, 1 Tim 6:10)

(171) Worry can't change your situation one iota, so why use all that precious energy to feed it? Why let your joy and happiness, your peace and contentment, vanish like precious water through sand? God has an answer to every situation, and those answers are embedded in His promises. Get your mind off yourself and locked onto His unsullied reputation to provide for you. Don't leave prayer until you are pulling your hair out, ignoring the mail, or unable to face anyone or anything! You walk by FAITH, not worry. Faith is your confidence. **(Gen 22:14, Ps 111:5, Acts 14:17, Matt 6:25-34)**

(172) The sport of Christians: When running a race, would you carry stuff you don't need or want which can only slow you down? Better to run without encumbrance, finish well and gain the prize. Give whatever hampers and burdens you to Christ; lay them all at the cross for *'His yoke is light.'* Deliverance, prayer, healing or surrender, do what you have to do because your freedom came at a heavy price. **(Matt 11:30, Gal 5:7, Heb 12:1)**

(173) Fear of death: I've been in a train accident, been blown up by terrorists, and once I almost drowned. By God's grace, I'm still here. God hasn't finished with me. He gave us all a destiny, a ministry to fulfil. When that's finished, we can go willingly home like Jesus, Paul, and millions of others. Stop being anxious about your life and live every moment for God and others. In Christ, there's no fear or mystery to bodily death only new life with Him. **(Rom 8:11, 2 Cor 5:17, 1 Thess 4:16, Heb 2:15)**

(174) God's Riches at Christ's Expense: We are continually saved by GRACE until called home. By no other name are we saved but Christ's; not puffed-up cathedral thinking, tradition, or religious formalities. We're declared righteous through faith not works. Strife and jealousy between the elect are born from comparing crosses and extolling self or corporate ambition. Never! One Christ, one church, and one cross for all! Watch out for grace robbers who seek to place you under law, guilt, and condemnation…most of them will be so-called Christians, and many of these, sadly, will be misguided leaders. **(Gen 15:6, Rom 3:21-31, Titus 3:5)**

(175) We're saved by grace not effort. The prodigal's brother was angry with the turn of events. Some Christians, often out of envy or frustration, stifle our joy and chain our freedom to a set of rules. They want a pecking order—follow their traditions to earn grace. King or beggar, repentance through faith is the key to conversion; grace is the gift it opened. Faith and works go hand in hand, but grace is the catalyst. Watch out for joy stealers.
(John 1:17, Rom 3:24, 5:2, 11:6)

(176) Are you haunted and hunted by things you did in the past? Give them to the one who can handle them and set you free—Christ. Don't be afraid. Determine to sort the past once and for all today. You can be forgiven and delivered of anything. Sort this matter through with God; get the devil off your back and live life to the full. Leave your millstones at the foot of the cross and walk the unburdened path of faith and hope, not turning back, neither to the left or the right. Let God's light shine the way, remember that His angels are your rearguard, and keep His words forever on your lips.
(Phil 3:13)

(177) Turn problems into challenges: God doesn't save us and then give us license to collect more baggage. His yoke is light. God's ways are perfect, and they lead to peace, joy, and total fulfilment . . . even in trouble. Wait and pray before an important or major decision, discern His will. Get to know what's best for life and peace in the eyes of God and we'll not have to lean on our own understanding, which is usually full of holes. God's direction leads to perfection in all things. Our utmost for His highest is our watchwords. **(Prov 3:5)**

(178) The things that rot the soul: Unforgivingness, bitterness, a haughty or religious spirit, lying, pride, unbelief, self-loathing, hate, works without faith, faith without works, lack of compassion, revenge, jealousy, gossip. . . and I'm sure we could all add to the list. Let God search your heart and shine His light on any area of darkness. Let Him set you free, break those chains. He loves you too much to let something slip and become an area for the devil to bind and torture you. **(Ps 139:23, Isa 61)**

(179) Calling and election: Since you've been joined to Christ and called to a specific purpose, you need to become like Christ in all you think, say, or do. To make a difference in the world, you must be in it but not of it. If people can't see Christ in you, then what hope is there for them to be set free like you? Your life is intertwined with every other, for we all come from Adam and Eve, yet as a Christian you are called to be the light of Christ to those who remain in darkness. Make your calling and election sure. Get right with God today and live for the salvation of others.
(John 8:12, Rom 12:12, 2 Pet 1:3-10)

GOD'S WORD

'Of the millions of books only one can breathe life into dead bones.'

(180) The holy words of the Bible aren't simply mere text on a page in a famous book full of nice stories and thought-provoking advice. God's words are packed with holy power—they are alive and kicking, they have a heartbeat, and they can miraculously change people and events. Let His Holy Spirit stir and release God's words in your life today with belief in the impossible through faith. **(Ps 68:35, Luke 10:19, Acts 6:8, Rom 1:16, 1 Cor 4:20)**

(181) God's word is empowered in you by the Holy Spirit. If you want to change 'anything' or 'anybody', know and use God's words precisely as He meant them to be used and not out of context. God's word is dynamite in holy hands, so check where you stand with God. There will be a person or situation that needs His life-changing word today, either directly from you or through your prayers. **(Ps 109:115, Prov 3:13, Luke 8:21, Heb 5:12)**

(182) As food is essential to flesh so God's word is to spirit. The Word is a powerful weapon. Feed on it even when you don't want to; it will sustain and build your faith, help you to change yourself and others through the power of the Holy Spirit. A soldier may not want to check his rifle every day, but he knows a fully functioning weapon will save his life in combat. Are you battling something, worn out, disillusioned, or wounded? Get into God's word. **(Isa 55:11, Matt 4:4, Eph 6:17, 2 Tim 2:15, Heb 4:12)**

(183) Stay in God's Word. We buy flat-pack furniture, grab a screwdriver, and the first thing we do is set the instructions aside because we know better than the manufacturer. That's the danger sign! *'The steps of the righteous are ordered by God.'* Best stick to the plan, one step at a time, and every part in the right place. Keep the plan close, referring to it at all times; live by it and it will produce life and health. **(Ps 37:23, 85:13, Prov 20:24, 2 Tim 2:15)**

(184) No good complaining to God that your faith is weak. *'Faith comes by hearing and hearing by the word of God.'* If you want more faith then get more word. *'It's impossible to please God without faith.'* That's why successful Christians, great healers, and powerful evangelists spend a lot of time with God? In His eyes, you are no different than them. An outworking faith leads to a blessed and successful Christian life. Start flexing your muscles of faith and see an amazing God in action. **(Rom 10:17, Heb 11:6)**

(185) Dust off your Bible. Religious rules bring sin, temptation, and bondage. You can't earn points with God. You're no greater or lesser than all of God's elect. Your righteousness is the same as Paul's or Billy Graham's—equal to all others. You cannot earn God's favour by attending church or being nice this week, more pious, giving more to charity. All you need has been provided for you in Christ. Faith matters and it comes by hearing (listening to/reading/meditating) God's word. *'Without faith you cannot please God,'* nor release all He has for you. Get the word in you and faith grows. **(Gen 15:6, Ps 18:20, Prov 21:21, Rom 1:17, 10:17)**

(186) If you want to stop facing trials alone and then blaming God because he didn't turn up at the right moment, then you must get into a proper relationship with Him. The only way is to study his instruction manual for life, the Bible. Let His promises act on you and you'll act on them. His word is His will. The Bible is life's road map; we ignore it at our peril, for *'God's ways are not our ways.'* There are no short cuts to a Godly life.
(Isa 55:8, John 14:6, 2 Tim 2:15, Heb 4:12)

(187) As our faith increases so too does God's power in our lives. All the instruction, guidance, and answers you need for life are in your Bible. God's holy manual is the blueprint to a content, happy, healthy, and well-lived life. His word is a solid foundation as you build the walls of faith, put on the roof of wisdom and knowledge. When the storms come your house will stand, and you will remember laying every brick and roof tile, word upon word, and His word will protect you. **(Matt 7:26, 1 Thess 2:4, 2 Tim 2:15)**

(188) Your spirit gives out whatever you put in. The way to stay positive and at peace is to feed your thoughts with sound Bible-backed truth despite how you feel, and then repeatedly confess the same to comfort, lift, repair, and strengthen your soul. Sow seeds of a positive acceptance and outlook—hope, like faith, is an act of your will; it will not happen through wishful thinking, luck, or magic. Remember, everything you do and think about produces after its kind, either for good or for bad, for peace or for torment. Press through and stay close to God's word whatever your circumstance. **(Phil 4:8-13)**

(189) You don't *have* to feel lonely and vulnerable; it's not a prerequisite of the Christian life. One of the devil's jobs is to isolate you for major attacks by feeding you falsehoods about your identity in Christ, in salvation, and what people think of you. He's the father of lies. You need to believe in God's (your true Father) word. Learn the appropriate verses, use them against the devil's whispers, and that will get your faith-shield up. *'Draw near to God and He will draw near to you.'* **(Eph 1, Heb 10:23)**

(190) Faith is to believe in something beyond human sight, when you can't see God's ultimate will for you. Get to that position and you're on a winner. *'Faith comes by hearing and hearing by the word of God.'* If you're frustrated at your faith-lack, then you've got to get into God's word and act on it. Note the impossible done throughout the Bible, especially in the book of Acts. Climb the little hills first, and then you can scale the mountains.
(Acts, 2 Cor 5:7, Heb 11)

(191) Satan feeds our minds with negative thoughts and hijacks the positive ones. In fact, he doesn't have to do much, simply flick a well-used switch and we're back on the old hamster wheel of misery, anxiety, despair, dread, and fear. God's word is medicine to body, mind, and soul. Forget to take His word regularly and we suffer, lose faith and hope, and we remain imprisoned by wrong thoughts and bad feelings. Let Christ restore your soul; let the Holy Spirit renew your mind with God's word. Live by faith, and think on *'. . . what is right, and good, and acceptable to God.'*
(Ps 23, Rom 12:12, 2 Cor 10:5, Phil 4:8)

(192) Demons need us to remain ignorant of them, making their destructive task easier. They want us to accept their lies and doubts about a living God; render our faith and core beliefs powerless. Their work is to repress and control people through sickness, fear, apathy, negativity, and complacency. Their prime objective: To keep you from God's truth! Determined prayer, active faith, and consistent fellowship are their main targets. Decide to do something about these attacks—fight back and overcome with the word of God. Live your life full of faith and hope, and in freedom as God intended. **(Matt 4:24, 10:8, Rom 8:37-39, Gal 5:1)**

(193) Stay close to God, and He'll fill your soul with self-acceptance, love, and laughter that will positively affect you and those around you—come hell or high water. The closer you get to God, the further your doubts and fears flee. Life pours over when you fill your days with His word instead of the corruptible things and worries of this imperfect world. Your own hopes and dreams are at best fleeting and at worse empty. God's promises give concrete hope, are as old as time, yet as fresh as morning dew, and they are always fulfilled. Live in God's word, and you'll live in His will for your life and times. **(Lev 26:13, Deut 10:12, Mic 6:8, James 4:8)**

(194) If I don't get before God when I wake, then my days are fraught with conflict in my mind and with others. Learn the discipline of fellowship with your creator. If you find that time difficult or boring, something is amiss, and you need to ask the Holy Spirit for revelation. Maybe you need to clear the decks of worry or a habitual sin. Whatever you have to change or give up, do so—the rewards are beyond measure.
(Deut 4:29, Ps 42:1, 69:32, Heb 11:6)

(195) Our God relationship breaks down when we stray from His word, become apathetic, or lose our first love. We need to check our *spiritual engine* with a regular 'pit stop'. Repentance and obedience keep us in tune; keep us running smoothly. If you don't put fuel in, you stand still. Fill up with the Holy Spirit, study the manual; be on the lookout for the tell-tale rattles and knocks that warn of impending trouble and costly bills.
(1 Cor 2:12, 7:1, Eph 4:30, 1 Thess 5:23, Heb 4:12)

(196) *'My refuge and fortress.'* Many trust in houses, banks, possessions, horoscopes, and often friends. Christians must weigh their safety and security on God's scales alone. His precepts never fail. His promises are never empty. His words never lie; they cannot abandon us, disappear, be found wanting, be lost or die. Every prayer in His will is answered one way or another. His WORD is solid rock in time of doubt, trouble, or loss. Read it today—lots of it. **(2 Sam 22:31, Ps 27:1, Ps 91)**

(197) Words contain power. Repentance and sin mirror blessings and curses. What we say is our responsibility, not God's. His word's already written. We can ignore or misuse His word to our peril and suffering, or we can use it to our joy and peace. Best we mark our words carefully, for they're carriers of life or death to us and others. Speak of what we fear most and it'll come upon us; rather speak truth and wisdom and they'll keep us. *'God's word is life and health to all flesh.'* **(Prov 4:22, Isa 40:8, Luke 11:28, Heb 4:12)**

BOLDNESS

'What is life without the courage to live it?'

(198) We flourish in life when we use our talents and gifts. Are you developing and using your natural and Godly gifting . . . then expect opposition from every quarter! The world and the church will not accept your talent and gifts on your say so; you'll have to exercise and prove them against all odds. For certain, the devil will fight tooth and nail to keep you barren and make your life seem pointless. Every part of us screams to give up when things get tough. People need what you have to give—persevere!
(Rom 5:3-4, 2 Thess 1:4)

(199) Milk or meat: If God gives you something, it's usually to do with helping others in the short or long run. Whatever He blesses you with, don't hold onto it for dear life but be willing to use or surrender it for others. The only thing you need in life is to be ready for the next move of God, both for your growth and to bless others. God will take care of all your needs so you can take care of His plan. **(Phil 4:19)**

(200) We ignore God's word at our peril, which is why many are troubled and sick among us. We can't walk with one foot in the world and the other in His Kingdom. Christ ransomed us, God adopted us, and the Holy Spirit guides us in constant repentance. Because the flesh, the devil, the world, peer pressure, and man-law says something is okay it doesn't mean it is when lined up with God's word. Learn to say no to what harms you.
(1 Cor 11:29-31, James 1:6-8)

(201) What use is faith without positive action, that golden nugget of enthusiastic certainty? If you pray with your expectations in your shoes don't expect answers. That's unbelief verging on arrogance. Paul said, 'The joy of faith was his'—from a prison cell! The joy set before Christ through the cross-horror was His realisation that man could be re-connected with God forever! No more enmity, just the joy of God's presence always. Simply believe, even when the odds are stacked against you. **(Ps 33:22, 39:7, 130:5, Lam 3:24)**

(202) The favour of God in everything you do is vital for success. Ask for His favour at work, home, school, university and on holidays, so that you *'will be successful at all you turn your hand to'* in His will for your life. Stand in line with the greats of the Bible. Men and women who had God's favour and changed situations, lives, and history! Constantly seek God's favour and walk tall through life. **(Ps 84:11, Prov 3:3-5, 2 Cor 6:2, 1 Pet 5:5)**

(203) Spiritual growth: Imagine it's a hot day and you race to the river. You enjoy the sunbathing, yet you refuse to go swimming. Instead, you remain on the bank envious of those enjoying the cool water. When the sun gets too hot, you get up and go home. Truth be told, you were scared of being out of your depth so you didn't even paddle, and you made your excuses. The Spirit says, "Fear not! Step into the river of life and swim." **(Ezek 47:1-5, Rev 22:1-2)**

(204) *Manna:* Has God called you? Many of the people God called were reluctant at first, some fearful. It isn't easy to go into the unknown in His name. There's no lengthy itinerary with God, He gives you enough directions and supplies for one day at a time. God's word is the food and drink of faith's success, without it the likes of Gideon and Joshua wouldn't have budged. When Christ calls to you, you need to obey and follow, or you'll rot and die inside. **(Exod 16:1-21, Judg 6:11-23, 1 Sam 10:21-23, Jer 1:1-10)**

(205) Gifting: What's happening to your spiritual gift? Yes, you do have one major one (possibly more as the Spirit moves). Is your gift growing, helping others and the church? Your gifting blossoms with use and alters lives, so don't ignore or bury it, let it rust, or be afraid of it. The devil squirms when you use your gift to help others grow and change. Seek wise council about your gift and its outworking. Your gift is as much part of you as your hands and feet. *'God's gifts and calling (His covenant promises) are irrevocable.'* **(Rom 11:29, 1 Cor 12:1-31)**

(206) Use your spiritual gift. We each have a spiritual gift. They are for the edification of our spirit-selves, the saving of the lost, and to encourage and build the church of believers. A person can play an instrument, but it only performs best when added to all the other instruments in an orchestra. Your fellowship needs your gifting. Why not find out where you fit in, and then exercise your gift. The Holy Spirit can also distribute all gifts to any given person at any time as He deems appropriate, but to you is given a personal one that fits you like a glove. Go bless yourself and others with your special gift. **(1 Cor 12:1-11)**

(207) *'He gives His angels charge over us.'* God is Spirit. His Holy Spirit is sealed in us. Angels are spirit forms who do God's business on our behalf for His Glory. We are flesh. Spiritual conflict requires spiritual forces. Our battles aren't against flesh and blood, but against principalities, demons, and every dark stronghold. ABIDE in God, and angels watch over, keep, and guard us as we fight the good fight. **(Ps 91, Eph 6:12)**

(208) *'A meal before my enemies.'* God blesses his own; feeds us when those around persecute us and mock our faith. His grace lays out the table while His love serves up peace and wisdom, longsuffering, and gentleness. His heart is hungry for those who mock us, preferring they come to know Him through your Christ-likeness rather than silence. Eat well! The good shepherd provides for his sheep even in the midst of hungry wolves. **(Ps 23)**

Barrie Kibble

RELIGIOUS DECEPTION
'Rat poison kills rats as surely as deceit kills truth.'

(209) Many Christians go through life believing healing and deliverance is only available through 'leaders'. Check your scripture. Jesus gives His power to ALL believers, and if you're baptised in the Holy Spirit you also can do what Christ did. If you reverently fear God and obey His commandments and run from sin, you've the same power that Christ had, for He lives in you through the Holy Spirit. Start moving in faith and persevere, for people need your help to set them free. Simply believe God's word and use it with holy authority. **(Matt 10:8, Luke 9:1-6, 10:19)**

(210) As a Christian, the only person you want in control is the Holy Spirit. Christ sets us free from all bondage. His Spirit can keep you free to be the unique individual God made. Watch out for the self-deceived or they'll deceive you. Heavy-shepherding: "Do what we ask or face restrictions; jump through our hoops or else." Beware of carrot-on-the-end-of-a-stick church authority. God is love—submitting to man-inspired religious laws and restrictions isn't love. **(Mark 7:8-9, Col 2:8)**

(211) Christ doesn't pursue ultimatums; they have no part in love's gentle process, but are all about fleshy control. You see this falsehood everywhere, especially in 'the church'. Christ died to set you free: see that you live that way and your joy will be full, your peace secure. Don't pursue others agendas which have nothing to do with God's will for you. Don't sell your integrity, water down your faith, or throw away your hope and calling to the schemes of people easily manipulated by the devil due to their error. Stand firm—*'The battle is the Lord's.'* **(1 Sam 17:47)**

(212) Deception is one of the major demonic spirits of the devil that feeds haughty, hardened, and proud hearts. We must remain in a constant state of love and repentance to rid ourselves of anything that sets us above others; makes us think we're right and all others are wrong. Even the most perceptive and knowledgeable among us can be deceived, believing that what we do for ourselves, the sake of others, or the church is done in the name of God. It's sound wisdom to keep a check on our motives. **(Ps 133, Eph 4:1-3)**

(213) The cost of integrity: The Devil was once an angel. Sin becomes acceptable and desirable when the rebellious among us believe that God is outdated and ought to catch up with our modern concepts of good and evil. We rewrite or re-interpret parts of God's word to make sin sociably acceptable then construct laws to protect those who practice it. We cannot re-crucify Christ or rewrite the Bible. *'God's word is the same yesterday, today and forever.'* Many miss out on God's blessing and favour because they take away or add to His word. Beloved, keep your eyes on Jesus and the narrow road. **(Heb 5:12, 13:8, Rev 22:18)**

(214) Spiritual compromise eventually costs us everything we hold dear. Many Christians abandon Biblical values and moral integrity. The compromise-misers water down God's word to appease others, including Spirit-empty church leaders; standing for what is Godly and overcoming every hurdle or falsehood becomes an inconvenience, comfort overrides character, and the path of least resistance replaces our witness to the lost. When God is mocked by Christians, the devil has a high time. Beloved, keep your eyes on Jesus and the narrow road. **(Prov 25:26, Rom 1:16-32, Heb 4:19, Rev 2:4)**

(215) It's sad and frustrating when Christians are bewitched by man-made religious dogma and cannot, through ignorance, compromise, or fear, expect more of God or be a living example of Christ in their town or city. We must endeavour to embrace the Holy Spirit and desire miracles and healing that will bring the lost to God. Our example is Christ, and He was uncompromising and radical because He knows the terrible cost for those who call Him Lord but refuse His life and works. Where do you stand with God today? **(Gal 3:1-3, Eph 4:14)**

(216) Being *radical* means dealing directly with a 'source or root.' Don't be scared of this word, but turn it to your advantage; welcome it; it gets rid of spiritual apathy, empty religion, false compassion, and false humility. Whatever issue arose, Christ dealt lovingly with the root, whether through healing, deliverance, wisdom, or righteous anger. He did everything the Father told Him to do without compromise. The devil loves powerless churches full of barren lives—don't help him to succeed. Be radical for God, but always sweeten it with love. **(1 Cor 4:21, Phil 3:10, 3 John 1:11)**

(217) Christ was radical because of what's at stake. Innocent, yet He gave His life freely, so *it is* a big deal. We don't know what hell will be like, but God knows. It breaks his heart to lose even one soul. Christ died to free humankind from sin, death and hell, to bring people back to God. You'll get radical, stop playing at church and going through the motions, when you get a revelation of the cross. **(Gal 5:1, Heb 12:1, Rev 3:16)**

(218) Harmony with God can't involve spiritual compromise. Jesus was compassionate yet radical. He had no time for *empty religion* or *temple abusers*. In fact, that was the only time He got truly angry. If you want to hamstring church growth, just implement everyone's views and agenda's and then squeeze in a bit of God's. Radical steps are needed to get the devil out of churches, and then we can give them back to God; then we can expect revival and a fresh move of Holy Spirit power! **(Prov 14:4, John 2:15)**

(219) When you KNOW God's calling on your life, you'll be greatly blessed, but you'll also meet stiff resistance, especially from those who worship *religion for religion's sake*. It's crucial that you listen to the Holy Spirit at all times and avoid the two greatest enemies of the church: compromise and apathy. Try and remain at peace with others if at all possible. Pray for those set against you so that God will enlighten them. Don't be moved—what God's set in motion He'll bring to fruition—for with the calling comes the anointing, and that's the ability and wherewithal to press through.
(Matt 16:6 & 12, 2 Tim 2:14, 2 Pet 2:1, 1 John 2:27)

(220) We Christians are all too often comforted by religious observance and gimmicks, convinced these are the norm—a couple of nice songs, a video, and hollow or puffed-up sermons. Few if any are healed, none delivered or saved, most left unstirred, unchallenged, and unchanged, and we remain powerless. That's not the kingdom of God! The world, the flesh, and the devil work hard to render you APATHETIC, FEARFUL, FAITHLESS, and UNFRUITFUL. Get Christ's passion for the cross back into your life, and then you can do what He did and more!
(Matt 16:10-12, John 14:12, Acts 17:22-25, Col 3:23)

Barrie Kibble

DEAD WORKS
'A flat battery powers nothing.'

(221) Religious rules bring sin and temptation. You can't earn points with God. You're no greater or lesser than all of God's elect. Your righteousness is the same as Paul's, Smith Wigglesworth's, or Billy Graham's—equal to all others. You cannot earn God's favour by attending church or being nice this week, more pious, giving more to charity. All you need has been provided for you in Christ. Faith matters and it comes by hearing (and reading/meditating) God's word. *'Without faith it is impossible to please God,'* or release all He has for you. Dust off your Bible. Get the word in you and faith grows. **(Gen 15:6, Ps 18:20, Prov 21:21, Rom 1:17, 10:17)**

(222) Is your Sunday any different than Monday? How's your spiritual resume? Are you safe within the walls of inaction and apathy? Are your thoughts and actions caught up with you or others? Does the worship in your church electrify your soul...is it conducted in Spirit and truth; take you into a wonderful place of inexpressible joy where your gift breaks forth and people are changed, healed, restored, forgiven . . . saved! **(John 4:23-24)**

(223) The Jezebel spirit: Beware the person or church that seeks control by flattery or enforced submission, "Our way or no way!" Don't be punished or penalised for simply being you—you've been set free! Don't fall into bondage again. *'There is no condemnation for those in Christ Jesus.'* Love is unconditional, doesn't demand, wave a stick, stifle your joy, or withhold any good thing. The true Christ-disciple and Christ-church accepts you as you are, accommodates and encourages you in your natural and spiritual gifts without forcing you to surrender or perform to a man-made agenda. **(Matt 23:1-4, Rom 8:1, Col 2:20)**

(224) If God's kingdom is in you on earth what do you think heaven will be like? Compare your church service with the eternal service in Revelation. If your church is apathetic to the Holy Spirit or just pays Him lip service . . . it's stagnating, and so are you! Start retaking territory from the devil; otherwise, under what justification do you still call yourself dead to flesh and alive in Christ? A vibrant and growing church is always in the front line of battle and doing amazing things to expand Christ's Kingdom despite hell's opposition.
(Isa 29:13, Matt 15:8-10, John 4:24, 1 Cor 14:26)

(225) A comfortable church that demands nothing of you is a powerless church. Consistent prayer will change your church from being impotent into a beacon for the lost. That brings the full release of the Holy Spirit, the eradication of compromise, and the death of people-power. Pray for worship in spirit and truth, sermons that leave you convicted and empowered, and a place you can see all the spiritual gifts in action. A radical church has a keen sense of evangelism without counting the cost, and she's held together with sacrificial love. **(Acts 1:14, 2:41-47, 1 Cor 14:12, 1 Pet 4:10, Rev 3:16)**

(226) Gifting: What's happening to your spiritual gift? Yes, you do have one major one (possibly more as the Spirit moves). Is your gift growing, helping others and the church? Your gifting blossoms with use and alters lives, so don't ignore or bury it, let it rust, or be afraid of it. The devil squirms when you use your gift to help others grow and change. Seek wise council about your gift and its outworking. Your gift is as much part of you as your hands and feet. *'God's gifts and calling are irrevocable.'*
(Rom 11:29, 1 Cor 12:1-31)

ATTITUDE

'Our beliefs, feelings, values, and the disposition to act in a certain way run amok unless they're bridled with love, compassion, mercy, and understanding.'

(227) *'Let your yes be yes and your no be no.'* All that lies in-between brings heartache, arrogance, pride, puffed up confidence, deception, perfectionism, loss of integrity, and all sorts of evil. If you call yourself a Christian adopt what is of Christ just as His Father has adopted you. From your mouth runs every wide road to hell or the single, narrow path to heaven. Choose once-for-all whom you'll serve—God or the devil, life or death. The tongue can produce a tiny spark that burns down a forest, or it can birth life, and plant seed that is good, pure and holy.
(Ps 34:13, Prov 10:19, Matt 5:37, James 3:5)

(228) *'Guard your tongue.'* What you say can build or break people and relationships. Negative words negate faith, hope, peace, and place God's blessings on hold. *'The power of life and death are in the tongue.'* Lies choke integrity, harm you and others; gossip dissipates good character and sows evil. False witness destroys the soul and bitterness rots the bones; anger brings walls down upon us, and judgement of others will return to us in full measure. Wisdom says: "Best think hard before you speak today." **(Prov 18:21)**

(229) Guard your tongue, for it has the power to build or destroy, and that choice starts in the heart. The tongue can kill, or it can be the balm to a thousand wounds. Control your tongue and you control your life. Keep your heart pure by forgiving others, not holding grudges and wanting revenge; don't judge or condemn people, and never gossip. Speak the best of others.
(Prov 10:20, 15:4, James 3:5)

(230) Let your words pour with love, encouragement, acceptance, forgiveness, blessing, and hope; let them reveal the gospel to the lost, bind the broken hearted, deliver and heal the wounded in body, mind and spirit. Let them be a balm, a living refreshment to parched souls; let them sow peace amidst hate, anger and adversity; let them destroy the fortress of worry, the concrete walls of anxiety, and bring light into darkness. Words are gold or dross, medicine or poison. Think hard before you unleash your tongue today. **(Prov 18:21)**

(231) Just as real mountains can be levelled with explosives, spiritual mountains can be shattered with praise. Some are convinced that the ways of God are foolish. Maybe they are to the earthly minded, the cynical, and faithless, but have you really tried the power of praise? Praise released chains and opened prison doors throughout the Bible; brought down Jericho's walls. Learn to praise until you overcome. Practice getting your eyes off the problem and onto God, then you'll find that *'all things are possible with God.'* Again, it's a habit, and you need to put some effort into it. Praise releases His power! **(Josh 6:4-5, Ps 100:4, Matt 19:26, Acts 16:25-26)**

(232) Praise: God's armies always have a choir at the head. Praise confuses and destroys the might, fortifications, and spirit of an enemy. Christian soldiers march to the rhythm of the word of God, and no other banner but love will do. What's the use of armour to a soldier if he doesn't put it on? Why go into battle ill-equipped and be wounded? Put on your armour and cry out with praise, draw the two-edged sword of the Holy Spirit and press forward against the enemy with certain victory in your heart and mind. Today's battles aren't yours to win, but the Lord's.
(Josh 5:15-20, 2 Chron 20:15, Eph 6:10-18)

(233) Praise knocked down the walls of Jericho, and it can do the same with your strongholds and problem situations. We've many weapons in our prayer arsenal; praise is the dynamite, powerful because it takes our eyes off ourselves and focuses on the Creator. Within minutes we feel better, lifted in faith, and oddly at peace. It's far easier for God to work when we get out of His way. Praise opens a highway for the blessings of heaven to travel down, whereas self-effort and worry slam shut the doors to His bulging warehouses. Try praise—taste and see the results for yourself. **(Josh 6:16, 1 Sam 17:47, Heb 11:30)**

(234) It's not easy to *'thank God in all things'* when your world's in chaos. Common sense says, "Don't be daft! Time to get angry, fed up, anxious; time to give up on this God-thing because it's not working." Praise shoves you firmly onto a spiritual plane, and things happen in heaven that'll affect you on earth. Christ's joy and peace are ours already, and both became part of us when we gave our lives to Him. Praising God frees these blessings; praise keeps all channels open and releases His power. **(Ps 146, Eph 5:20, Col 2:7, James 1:2-4)**

(235) Make today special: Love and accept yourself, enjoy everything you do. Refuse to be upset by others—they have problems too. Encourage someone, especially if they're a thorn in your side. Think good thoughts, and do whatever you set your hand to with all your might. Stop fussing and worrying about stuff, take it all to God and leave it there! Practice and service your Christianity each day and you'll become more like Christ; you'll learn to live in peace, joy, and hope, whatever the circumstance. **(Eccles 9:7, Isa 41:13, Col 3:23)**

(236) About Getting Even: *'Love your enemies and pray for those who persecute you.'* Such prayer frees God to deal with them His way—not your way. Check to see if your motives are pure. **(Matt 5:44)**

(237) One of the secrets to a life well-lived is serving, putting others before self, and concern about others needs over and above our own even when it costs. Watch over others as God watches over you, and if you've got what people need, give it freely. *'Give and it shall be given to you, filled up, pressed down and overflowing.'* Willing obedience to God brings blessings instead of curses—obedience to sin, fleshy lusts, and desires brings curses instead of blessings. You're reading one of the major answers to a satisfied life, and to days full of joy, peace, and plenty. **(Mark 10:45, 1 Pet 4:10)**

(238) When facing seasons of financial difficulty, it seems totally illogical to give ten-percent of our first fruits to God. We bluster and reason and tell Him why it's impossible. Yet we wonder why we struggle with lack; we doubt God truly cares about our situation. Elijah asked a widow to share her final meal with him as starvation stalked her door. She said yes despite fear, common sense, and what her eyes saw. Immediately, she locked into a divine, endless supply source! God loves to do the foolish and impossible. He strengthens our faith in His provision, especially when we need it most. We need to learn in the tough times that tithing unlocks God's warehouses. **(2 kings 4:1-7, Mal 3:10, 2 Cor 9:7)**

(239) Don't take fasting lightly. Fasting is a personal or joint sacrifice giving glory to God, not to get His ear, but to be obedient to suppressing the flesh in order to strengthen the spiritual roots of worship, prayer, and spiritual warfare. To fast is to deprive the body of food for a fixed time and to spend that time in prayer, thanksgiving, and worship. Fasting is a major discipline that invariably entails hardship. God isn't mocked. Don't expect a spiritual reward for a fleshy attempt at pleasing church, self, or people. **(Matt 6:16-18)**

(240) If we engage in pre-marital sex we sow retribution and misery because we sold out our moral high ground for sugar-coated sin, and someone *always* gets hurt. If we lay with another person who's not our wife or husband we still become one spirit with them, and someone *always* gets hurt. In both cases, we receive part of their souls into us; we don't get to choose which part, the devil does that. Then the devil waits his time before he strikes—and he always strikes! Best talk to God today and put matters right. **(Prov 6:32, Matt 5:28, 15:18-20, Rom 3:13, 1 Cor 6:12, Eph 5:3, Col 3:5)**

(241) *'BE OF GOOD CHEER.'* The devil's job is to ensure you never forget your failures. He has every bit of dirt on you; he hacks your mind and spreads it on the front page of your daily existence. Lies, anger, filth, past horrors and hurts, betrayal, theft, thoughts you think that no one else would dare think. But Christ now stands advocate for you in the courts of judgement. He paid the price, took full punishment, redeemed you, and saved you from permanent death with hope in this life and a place in heaven. That's grace. That's the price of the cross, Jesus in exchange for all your evil. **(Prov 17:22, 1 John 2:1-2)**

(242) *'A cheerful disposition is good for the health.'* Adhering to God's precepts, His commands and will—living a Godly life—is good for the health. Holy awe and reverent respect (natural fear of sinning against God), honour, and giving Him all the glory, will bring long life in full measure. Hearing and acting in faith on God's wisdom (His word) brings length of days.
(Prov 4:20-22, 15:13, 17:22)

(243) Surrender: God displays His glory through imperfect people. Accept your limitations. His strength powers through your weakness. Unless you surrender all to Christ, you'll win few battles because self-knowledge is fragile, a hindrance, and fulfilling your calling will be fraught with snares and traps. Stop skirting the cemetery and jump into the grave of total surrender—fully embrace the power of the Holy Spirit. **(2 Cor 12:9)**

(244) Many stories fly about demon-driven ministries and ministers. Attacking each other isn't pure Christianity, it's of the devil. He thrives on discord. Agree with scripture: *'Whoever is not against us is for us.'* Paul makes a sensible point based in the love, compassion, and the grace of God: *'Some preach Christ for self or gain, but rejoice anyway that Christ is preached.'* Keep your walk and faith simple, concentrate on what Christ did. There are no perfect churches, not even the one you're in. You were saved for Christ-likeness, not man-made institutions. Guard your heart. Keep your hope and vision clear. **(Mark 9:38-39, Phil 1:12-18)**

(245) Worldly, fleshy love is selfish and ends in torn hearts and broken dreams because it seeks its own. Contaminated love is an 'iron curtain' that splits soul and spirit and renders life impotent. God's love begins and takes root in repentance and salvation. The mystery is that such love never ends; it brings mercy, hope, peace, joy, freedom, healing, and forgiveness; it delivers from selfishness, false ambition, immoral desires, hate, anger, hopelessness. God's love must begin in you before it pours out to others; it brings an acceptance as to who you really are—then it frees others to be the same. **(1 Cor 13)**

(246) Christians must never judge for they're saved by grace: 'God's Riches at Christ's Expense'. Find the best in the worst of others; search for it in the narrowest and darkest streets and alleys of peoples' personalities, for you're a sinner saved by grace. If you want to reveal to others what Christ has revealed to you, accept people as they are and let the Holy Spirit work through you, through your unconditional love and your deep compassion of their needs. If others don't see a Christ-likeness in you...then you are the *'blind leading the blind.'* **(Matt 7:1-5, 2 Cor 12:9)**

(247) We need to stop blaming the devil for everything and take responsibility for our thoughts and actions. A truck-load of misery comes from fleshy works. If you walk in the Spirit, you'll feel and experience life, but if you walk in the flesh, you'll experience misery and barrenness. Don't blame the devil for your negative moods and treatment of people, lack of healing, unforgivingness, unanswered prayer, and unmet needs. God knows all about you. He does exactly what He wants to do, exactly when He wants to do it, and with only our best for His highest in mind—the flesh has to die to clear all paths to Heaven. **(Ps 139:23, Isa 55:8, Gal 5:16, Heb 3:1)**

(248) If you forgive those who hurt and abuse you, you've found the keys to free soul and spirit. If you trust God whatever the circumstance, you'll have peace. If you can see reason and purpose in everything that befalls you, you'll be chained to hope. Happiness is fleeting, but God's joy is permanent: *'A cheerful disposition is good for the health.'* If you keep your life unstained from sin by constant repentance, you'll walk with God and have His ear like Enoch, King David, and Paul. If you can find acceptance, love, space, and encouragement for every person you meet they'll see Christ in you. **(Gen 5:22-24, Rom 8:28, Phil 2:1-11)**

(249) Concentrate on the best in others instead of the worse, and they'll reciprocate. We adopt attitudes, trust in actions and defences that we have grown to accept and believe are the norm; they make us what we are at the moment; we feel secure with them. Others react differently because they have a different set of coping attitudes and values. God accepts you for what you are, so accept others for what they are. Let God change them—and you! That saves a lot of misunderstanding, broken relationships, and untold trouble. **(Matt 7:12, Luke 6:28, Rom 14:3)**

(250) Unrealistic expectations make you miserable. As long as you're on this planet, you'll experience problems. Christian or not, young or old, nobody gets a free pass. Learn to be realistic. You'll always have to deal with things you don't like about yourself; then there's difficult people and unpleasant situations. Your attitude to all these matters will determine whether or not you learn to cope with, and enjoy, God's gift of life.
(John 6:33, 10:10, Col 2:17, 1 Pet 4:1-19)

(251) Think carefully about what you ask for. God knows what's best for us and when to give it. We often think He has to give us what we need immediately. We beg, cry, and moan because rationally it makes sense to have our every need met now! We often force the issue, grasp the temporal fix, the second best, use our worldly faith, and regret it later. We get into all sorts of trouble, hurt, and upset when we engineer those needs. Long-suffering, patience, and trust are not the hard way. They are the best way for true growth, faith, health, and peace of mind. **(Matt 6:5-8, John 14:14)**

(252) 'Never let your emotions drive your decisions.' This maxim is so relative to the way we shape our thoughts and reactions. People cannot help but hurt us because they get hurt too. How we handle that destructive force is vital to our peace, joy, and sanity. On-the-spur or knee-jerk reactions can ruin a good thing or a precious relationship. Remember, it's difficult, if not impossible, to untangle what we say or do. **(Prov 29:11)**

(253) Patience: Moses got fed up waiting for God to release his enslaved countrymen. He ended up in a wilderness for 40 years after murdering one of the slavers—from prince to nobody in a few inglorious seconds. Are you fed up waiting for God to act on his promises and think you need to help Him? That's the danger sign! His timing is perfect, and it's not just to bless you but others too. Wait for Him; it will save much grief and heartache. **(Isa 40:31, Heb 11:1, 2 Pet 3:8)**

(254) We flourish when others encourage us, pat us on the back, pick us up, dust us off, and tell us to keep going despite the odds. Others flourish when we mirror these most excellent virtues. We must do all our good acts out of a sense of joy, out of putting others first. *'What you reap so shall you sow.'* When we fit in with God's universal truths, all things are possible; it's then that our stumbling faith becomes an aggressive faith. **(Hosea 6:3, Gal 6:7- 8, Phil 3:13-15)**

(255) You flourish when you pursue your natural talent(s) and Godly calling. Doing whatever you are good at, and anointed to do, bring contentment, peace, joy, and satisfaction. People who are happiest with themselves and life trust in God. They're willing to overcome their fears and climb the towering mountains of disappointment and doubt to fulfil their God-given purpose. They furrow the fields of rejection and failure, burn off the weeds, break the sods and plant hope—in due season they produce a crop. Talents and gifts are perfectly tailored to each individual, and people do best through the minefields of life when they doggedly pursue what God made them for. **(Rom 5:3-5, Heb 12:1, 2 Pet 1:5-7)**

(256) Christians are fickle at times. Desperate to see friends, relatives and strangers saved, healed, delivered, or restored, but not desperate enough to stick close to God and grow in faith to see it accomplished. We go where He tells us and to whom He points out, and we pray or lay hands on them that they be delivered, healed, restored, and set free. Christ didn't avoid or play about with the cross; He got nailed to it. He stuck close to Father; did His will at all times, whatever the cost. **(Ps 51:12, Gal 6:9, Heb 10:35)**

(257) Life's like a carousel; you enjoy the ride and think you're going somewhere, but it runs in circles; you see the same view of people and things, and it breaks down a tad too often. Occasionally, you need to ride the ghost train or get your heart-thumping on the roller-coaster. The real fun of the fair is to have pushed yourself beyond your limits, your comfort zone, and hammered the bell, faced your fears, and enjoyed the scares. If you've bought a Christian ticket, make the most of it: Walk by faith; take calculated risks—look for and witness miracles! **(Eccles 11:1-6, Matt 19:29)**

(258) Fill up your life with God and He'll fill up your life with heaven. Pour yourself into others and His Spirit will pour into you. Take your mind off self, think of others needs and God will supply *all* your needs. Let troubles strengthen, not break you. Never, ever, let go of hope despite all that appears to the contrary. Stop sinning. Master fear before it masters you. Guard your tongue with grace and love. Flee from those who gossip, curse God, and plot evil. Bad company brings a counterfeit joy that eventually kills your soul and rots your bones. Forgive when it hurts, and keep your vows. Hold fast to faith, and she'll carry you home. **(1 Cor 13, 15:33)**

(259) Of all places, the cross is where we sort things out amicably with others in a spirit of forgiveness, gentleness, and kindness. There are struggles in all areas of life, yet how we handle them under God is the crucial factor that epitomizes the very core of unity and faith: Christ's banner of love. God is always moving forward, and we should listen carefully and move with Him, or change lanes if He shows us a different direction. **(Song of Sol 2:4, Eph 4:32)**

(260) Sin forms habits, so falling into it becomes easy, commonplace, and we fool ourselves into believing lots of abnormal things are normal—normal to be agitated, miserable, and hopeless? Unless we surrender those areas of sin to the Holy Spirit and let Him renew our minds, we forfeit God's blessings in our lives. Bad habits can be replaced with healthy ones, which will restore our peace and joy, and above all, God's favour. Confront sin before it drags you deeper into its bottomless pit.
(Prov 10:16, Rom 6:23, 12:2)

(261) *'We reap what we sow.'* We can't change the universal laws of God. Everything reproduces after its kind. Faith begets faith—fear begets fear. Truth begets truth—lies beget lies, and so on. Think and act on what's good, and pure, and holy, and help others. Look for the good in self and others. Bridle the tongue and exercise the ears. *'Seek you first the kingdom of God and everything else will be added to you.'* **(Gal 6:7-8)**

(262) We waste valuable time and energy deciding who we like and don't like; it determines our emotional response to ourselves and others. God looks for a pure heart and inward treasure. A home needs windows and doors for a happy life. Don't dwell on appearances or impressions, but on the good substance in yourself and others. He made us as we are and others as they are for reasons beyond our immediate understanding. We find true acceptance of ourselves when we look out for others. Focus on others needs and trust God to meet yours.
(Matt 5:43-45, Luke 10:27, John 13:34-35, Rom 13:8, Gal 5:14)

(263) Do you want to look and feel your best? Then clothe yourself with Christ. God sees you differently than you so often see yourself. He can see His Son in you; He's able to look upon you, welcome you into the holy of holies because of the price His Son paid. God sees you as perfect going on perfect, as He refines you to be fit for purpose. Don't forget your robes of righteousness today. See yourself through God's eyes. **(Rom 13:14, Gal 3:27)**

(264) Stress: Instead of wrestling with everything that comes your way, why not change how you think and approach the vagaries of life? A change in attitude takes an act of will, but with the help of the Holy Spirit you can renew your mind and find God in everything you do and think. You can start to accept that people say the wrong thing, trouble happens, and you will make mistakes, that people and circumstance will let you down. Every day is good if you aren't getting beaten like Paul or crucified upside down like Peter—go count your past blessings.
(Lam 3:22-24, Rom 12:2, Eph 4:23)

(265) Inspiration without commitment won't get you far, nor will faith without patience. You must first believe in the reliability of the promise giver and trust for the answers. You have to say, "I'm going to stand come hell or high water" and "I refuse to dig up the promise-seeds God has planted." Agreement with God's promises is easy, but patience for a harvest is tough unless we stand firm against the devil's schemes. **(Gal 5:7, James 4:7, 1 Pet 5:8)**

(266) Stop bemoaning your life. Change your bad attitudes toward yourself, everything you do, and everyone you meet. Reassess your goals and hopes and bring them in line with your gifts, talents, and God's plans. Don't *'kick against the goads,'* discipline is essential to joy and contentment. Forgive your enemies, yourself, and above all God. It's time to move on and embrace life, and that includes accepting and burying the past. Live again, for life is so terribly short and you have so much to accomplish! **(Matt 5:1-14)**

(267) Longsuffering: Cut-up in the car, awkward neighbours, bad manners, and ignorant or rude people can plunge us into intolerance. Difficult as it may be, we need to see people as God sees them. *'That none should perish but all come to glory.'* Count to ten the next time you're about to explode, and try and understand what drives those who upset you; remain calm and go the extra mile for their soul's sake. No, it isn't easy, but it is possible. **(Matt 5:13-14 & 43-44, 18:2-5, Rev 15:4)**

(268) *'His truth is your shield.'* Have you noticed that when you speak the truth you feel good and your conscience is unburdened, even when it's uncomfortable? That's called integrity, and God's people will meet Kings because of it. God's truth is His word, watertight and steadfast; the source of every good thing. Truth protects us in a world where falsehood is applauded and honesty despised. Don't betray your righteousness or lower your shield of truth. **(Ps 91, 119:142, Prov 8:8)**

(269) *'I will fear no evil.'* If you have accepted God as head of your life, there's nothing else you need than the creator of mankind on your side, totally committed to you, and looking out for you. *'He who is in you is greater than he who is in the world.'* To disarm the enemy of faith, you must love unconditionally, keep repentance close to your heart, and follow God's precepts. The devil seeks to steal life, destroy mind and body. Keep your thoughts stayed on God, and do not give ground to the devil. *'If God is for us, who can be against us?'* **(Ps 23, 1 John 4:4, Rom 8:31)**

(270) *'We reap what we sow'* is an unavoidable truism; it's an unwritten law of the universe, and it's Biblical. You cannot run from it, go over it, around it, only through it. You can't deny it, remove it, or pretend life isn't like that. Think carefully about your words and actions. If you sow an ill wind you'll reap a whirlwind. If you sow good thoughts about others, good words, and good deeds you shall reap of the good. **(Matt 7:1, Gal 6:7-8)**

(271) Temptation says, "Just do it; worry about it later." Temptation acted upon is to temporarily enjoy what permanently harms us. Wilfulness and rebellion are the flesh saying we know better than God. Temptation sneaks through the left open doors of unchecked desires and needs; comes through anger and hurt, unforgivingness, tiredness, desperation, lust and pride; comes to infect, poison, rot and destroy the good in us, all that's worthwhile, precious, all peace, hope and self-control. Christ was a mere man like us, yet He resisted temptation. Start to refuse the desires that bring death not life. **(1 Cor 10:13, 2 Cor 10:5, Matt 26:41)**

(272) Pride precedes captivity: Humility births freedom. Pride puffs up, causes factions, self-deludes, warps truth, and puts self first. Pride ends in heartache and tears. Humility puts others first, keeps us real, on the path to achieve what we're made for, to accept and rub shoulders with the lowly and kings alike. Humility is: not being crushed when we fail, but knowing we can try a thousand times again. Humility is always peace, and peace always finds a way. True greatness comes from a humble heart.
(Prov 11:2, 16:18, 29:23, 1 John 2:16)

(273) Each of us is called to a God-given ministry, and He seals in us the gifts and talents to complete the course; He also gives us the ability and the anointing to do it. Armed and equipped, we step out in faith with the sure hope and confidence that, *'what He has called us to do, He is more than able to complete.'* We can't escape trials; they're a natural part of the refiner's fire and can make us stronger depending on our attitude. Everyone takes the journey of life, but if God is our guide, we'll inherit eternal life at mortal life's end. That's the Father's promise to his beloved—His guarantee, and no man, situation, set back, or demon can take away what is written!
(Rom 11:29, Phil 1:6)

(274) We're not only born with natural talents, but also a spiritual gift to use and a ministry to fulfil. Without God, brute force and talent might get us through life, and we might leave worldly footprints, but in time, they will disappear. With God, nothing's wasted, all welded together to forge a memorial plaque of no regrets and total fulfilment. Everyone will see our spiritual footprints and recall that we passed this way thanks to the good fruit we left behind. **(Matt 12:33, Luke 6:43, John 15:16)**

(275) God can demolish the toughest strongholds in your life and in the lives of others, as well as revive a spiritually dead or struggling church. Therefore, only you can frustrate yourself and blunt your vision if you continually take back control of every situation, person, and problem. Never say nobody cares, because God does, and He's waiting to prove it to you if you'll let go and let God. **(Ps 89:40, 2 Cor 10:4)**

(276) Compassion: Blessed are those who recognise God, Christ, and the Holy Spirit, and who attend to the needs of others. At the final accounting, the only thing that'll count is the parts of yourself that you sacrificed for no reward to make others rich in Christ. Wherever you go, whoever you meet, you will only be seen for that which you have freely given away. On that last journey of journeys, all you'll take is all that you gave, and it'll either be nothing or it'll be everything.
(John 17:3, Rom 14:9, 1 Cor 2:2, 6, Phil 1:21, 3:8)

SELF-WORTH
'A mirror is useless if you're blind inside.'

(277) If you think no one cares or loves you, Christ does, and He's prepared to love you unconditionally and watch over you forever. That's despite whatever you've done in the past, which, amazingly, God chooses never to recall. *'He removes our sin as far as the east is from the west.'* The Father loves you unconditionally. Check His word . . . nowhere does it say that those who call on His name will be ignored, shunned, punished, remain sick or full of fears and demons, be condemned, or live without forgiveness, hope, and renewal. Accept Christ and let the Holy Spirit have all of you! **(Deut 31:8, Ps 103:12, 1 John 1:9)**

(278) Think you're too fat or too thin, ugly, useless at everything, worried about what others say, not up to any task, fail people, cannot form relationships...stop! God made you as you are for a reason, and He accepts and loves His workmanship. Self-punishment, misery, despair, and pity-parties are not part of His blueprint for you. Accept yourself and stop finding ways to hide or escape from His choice. You'll find every answer for your life and hope in His word, not in self, the world, or others opinions. **(John 15:19, Rom 8:33, Eph 1:11, 1 Thess 1:4, 1 Pet 1:2, 2:9)**

(279) Change the bad perceptions you hold about yourself, others, and the world, and your circumstances will change for the better. People will start to smile at you; see you in a new light. Your old negativity will radiate positivity. Make a decision today, once and for all, to stop hating all of God's workmanship. Break the treadmill of selfish moods, attitudes, and actions. People need what you have to give. Get your mind and eyes off your fullness and onto the emptiness of others—no one can do it for you. If you're truly His, God is always with you, but don't expect Him to attend your self-pity parties; and stop mixing with faithless or Godless people. Take back your life! **(Deut 31:6, Ps 9:10, 1 Cor 15:33)**

(280) Stop knocking yourself—the devil thrives on it. His demons hold parties in honour of your self-loathing and misery. They fashion giant placards in your mind: pointless, ugly, useless, stupid. They stir up fears and anxieties, and bake huge cakes to feed your self-pity. Their job is simple: to remind you of your faults and failures in order to keep you from enjoying the freeing truth of God's word. Look outward, not inward. God loves and accepts you as you are. People need you and what you have to give, so don't give the devil your precious self-worth. **(Isa 41:9, Eph 4:27)**

(281) You'll never come second if you put God and others first! God wants your worst to fashion your best. You haven't lived unless you've died to self; you'll never be satisfied if you've not tasted Christ. Don't let the world or any person-pleasing apathy or barren, ineffective church trample your gifts. Your gift(s) are the miracles of your life hid with Christ to encourage the church, help others, and save the lost. You don't know what you really need until you find God in your pain and emptiness. Get out of sin's darkness and into His light. Let go—let God. Surrender, and find victory in all you do. **(Isa 54:8, 1 Cor 12:1-11, James 4:7-10)**

(282) If you refuse to let go of the past, it won't let go of you. The strongest wall isn't dry stone but bricks and mortar. A dry wall has gaps and is easily knocked down. A solid wall is cemented, immovable, the weight distributed across all the bricks. That's the difference between accepting bits of what God says about you in His word and all of what He says. Your past belongs at the cross or it will hamstring your future; your past includes the mess or disappointments of today, too. God doesn't make His word different for different folk, it's the same freedom, forgiveness, and grace for everyone—everyone includes you! **(Gal 5:1, Eph 6:9)**

(283) "Lord, deliver me from me." We often give the devil much credit when we put ourselves down, punish ourselves, and hold to a low opinion. We constantly sin or blame God for stuff that has nothing to do with Him, or we lay our faults and gripes at His door. We need to take responsibility not only for our actions, but also to applying God's word in our lives. Live by God's precepts if you call yourself a Christian. **(Isa 43:18, Gal 6:5)**

(284) Tell yourself enough that you are useless, things always go wrong, you are going to be ill, life sucks, nothing ever good happens to me, and guess what – you get what you asked for. YOU control your thoughts, and your words are either full of life or full of death. Thoughts are born in the mind, settle in the heart, and come out the mouth—every word you speak has a measure of faith behind it, for good or ill! God wants to renew your mind, purify your heart, and give a positive faith to your words through His life-changing word. **(Ps 139:23, Mark 7:21, Heb 3:1, James 3:5-6)**

(285) Saul persecuted and helped to murder Christians until he met with the living God on a dusty road on his way to eradicate more of us. By grace, God turned him into a powerful man for the gospel. From Saul to Paul, religious zealot to Christ's apostle—a permanent change. Do you think Paul could have achieved what he did unless he chose to crucify his past? For goodness sake, forgive yourself, and then you can move on. **(Acts 9:1-5, Luke 9:62, Phil 3:13)**

(286) *'The Lord is my shepherd.'* Sheep follow each other onto barbed wire and into ravines, become easily lost, often panic. If one gets stuck on its back due to its thick wool, it dies because it can't right itself. That's why they need a shepherd to care for and guide them; protect them against predators; to be there sunshine or storm. Sheep may all look the same, but only a shepherd knows each particular one by name. **(Deut 31:8, Josh 1:5, Ps 23, John 10:3)**

(287) Accept once and for all how God sees you or you'll live in misery wishing you were happier, more attractive, more intelligent, etc. Leave the past behind or you'll be constantly looking back. You won't change anything by worrying—go on, try it for a week! You won't change anything with regret or guilt either! Live in the now and like yourself. Appearances, feelings, and moods are deceptive and fleeting. Work this through with God and start to love yourself. **(Matt 6:27-34, Luke 12:25, Gal 5:22)**

(288) Accept yourself: Before the cross I am as nothing. I say of Christ, have mercy on me for there is so much I do not understand. And Christ says, "I don't see what you see but what My Father sees, and He's well pleased". And I shout again, "I don't understand." And my beloved replies, "It's not for you to understand but to simply believe."— "My God", I say, "Is it that simple?" And Christ says, "Yes, now and for ever."
(Jer 33:3, Eph 1:1-23)

Barrie Kibble

SELF-DISCIPLINE
'A person who doesn't tie their shoelaces is headed for a fall.'

(289) Self-discipline is extremely important; the lack or dereliction of it creates problems both for you and others. Undisciplined behaviour incurs loss of self-respect. To others, an unfulfilled promise or transaction is like receiving a present and finding nothing in the box. People will treat you as you treat them, i.e. always turn up late and people peg you as unreliable; they won't take you seriously. Trust and respect are earned by our integrity to keep our word. God does exactly what He promises—we need to do the same. **(Prov 12:1, Phil 1:27, 2 Thess 2:17, 2 Tim 1:7, Heb 12:11)**

(290) Jealously guard your walk of faith: Keep an eye on your seed or the crows will steal it. Keep your thoughts pure or they'll bring you shame and heartache. Work at good relationships or they'll rot and die. End bad relationships before they end you. Rushing into anything places a millstone around your neck. Living in debt is a snare that suddenly snaps shut. Trusting to your own reasoning is like walking on paper-thin ice. Self-promotion is like dancing in a minefield. Making life choices and then trying to get God's blessing on them is like swimming in treacle. Planting and watering God's word in your heart is life, health, and prosperity. **(Prov 4:23, Luke 8:21, Heb 1:1-3)**

(291) Give the devil an inch and he'll stretch it a mile. He whispers how proud we should be, how better we are than others, how right we are, how we could achieve so much alone, how others don't understand us. He convinces us that we are right and others are wrong. He says, "Sin a little for you're only human" and, "Poor you, God expects too much." Be vigilant. The devil *is* a roaring lion: his teeth *are* razor-sharp, and his bite *is* bone-deep. Repent, make a stand, hold your ground, and then take the fight to our common enemy. Stick close to God! **(John 8:44, 1 Pet 5:8)**

(292) Has God asked you to do something but you've ignored Him? Has the blessing gone or the Holy Spirit's power lessened? Why kick against the goads when you only harm yourself? Better to be obedient—it *is* for your own good, joy, and peace. Whatever He asked of you *is not* only for your blessing, but also so others can be blessed. Non-compliance might not be an obvious sin to you, but disobedience has far-reaching consequences. Trust God, and do what He says. He knows best for your best.
(Josh 7:1-12, Acts 26:14, Heb 4:6)

(293) God's more interested in our character than our comfort. Comfort's good and necessary, but at best it's still temporary. Character shapes and affects everything we do, everyone we meet, what we say, and how we react. We learn to persevere through trials, however debilitating or fearful. We hold our temper, face our fears; we don't run away from responsibility, curse, rage, or seek revenge. We forgive before hate turns us bitter. This is how we grow, how our character is built, how we become more like Christ and draw people to Him. No of course it isn't easy, but be assured that it does get easier. **(Ps 11:7, 25:21, 97:11, Prov 16:17)**

(294) *'You will reap what you sow.'* The words you say and the acts you do *will* return to you in full measure. If they're for good, then good shall repay good, but if they're for evil, then evil shall repay evil. Be careful what you say; be wary of what you turn your hand to, for God's universal and everlasting words cannot be altered or brushed aside, nor should they be taken lightly. Best think and pray before you act or speak today. **(Gal 6:6-8)**

(295) When the Old Testament priests prepared the alter sacrifices they had to keep the ravens away. When farmers plant seeds, they use devices to keep birds away. When we plant faith-seeds, we need to ensure nothing and no one can destroy or steal them. We need to stay alert; our mind in the word, our eyes on Jesus. Paul didn't speak of the *armour of God* in casual passing, but that we should put it all on and keep it all on. Ignore one piece, and we weaken the other parts. **(Eph 6:10-18)**

(296) Patience is tough to master. Learning to wait on God's timing is essential to our faith, joy, and peace. A quiet confidence is forged by patience—knowing precisely when to act and speak are two of her children. There's a God-given time for all things under the sun. While waiting, we don't worry, fuss, and stamp our feet but we get on with a life hid with Him; totally dependant on God as patience matures our character into Christ-likeness.
(Eccles 3:1, Jer 17:7, Eph 3:12, Heb 10:35)

(297) If we can conquer ourselves, we can conquer anything. Self-control guards the soul and mind from scars and unwanted baggage. We become slow to speak and quick to listen. Fast to care rather than judge, and quick to repent and forgive. We learn to be totally reliant on God's word and totally trust in his promises. We live each day for Christ without counting the cost, willing to give our life for Him because He gave His for us.
(Prov 3:5-6, Gal 2:20, Eph 6:12, Phil 1:21, 2 Tim 1:7)

(298) Christ calls us to compassion not pity, understanding not judgement, and knowledge not ignorance. He calls us to passion not apathy, love not hate, long suffering not a quick fix. He's always calling but will we listen, and then will we act. What sacrifice mirrors His…none, but that you humbly walk at His side and do His bidding that all should know Him as Christ crucified, Christ risen, and grace personified.
(Exod 33:19, Matt 9:36, 20:34, Eph 4:32, Col 3:12, 1 Pet 3:8)

(299) Without fellowship, the Christian life is powerless; all has to be done in our own strength. This is exactly what the devil wants. We become impotent, barren, and ineffectual, Christian in name only! No soldier enters battle alone but with his squad, each one looking out for the other; each with the right mindset and equipment. A spiritual hospital awaits those who go it alone and lack the right weapons. God made us to be with others of like mind. **(Acts 1:14, 2:42-47, Heb 10:25)**

(300) *'Green pastures and still waters.'* Times of rest and relaxation are vital to our health and mood, and they recharge our batteries. Take or make time for your favourite way to relax; sustain a balance in life or it'll become unbalanced. As God's word is for spirit and soul, rest and fun are for mind and body. Take care of yourself. The good shepherd knows his sheep need rest, food, drink, and a time to play. **(Exod 34:21, Ps 23)**

(301) *'Your rod and staff comfort me.'* Without discipline and direction our lives would be aimless, chaotic. (1) Prayer is a vital self-discipline that brings light where there's darkness in situations and people. (2) Committing our way to the Lord is a wise habit if we're to stay on the right path; our eyes fixed on the cross. The good shepherd gently corrects, guides, and reassures his sheep with rod and staff. **(Ps 23)**

HOPE
'Life without hope is a precious seed left to rot.'

(302) "Oh God I believe, please help my unbelief." God knows what our every need is, but He always answers according to our faith. Step out today with faith in your words married to God's word and plant those seeds of expectation. Get rid of words laced with worry, fear, dread, and anxiety. *'Without faith it is impossible to please God.'* If you need more faith, ask Him. *'He will withhold no good thing from those He loves.'* **(Ps 84:11, Mark 9:24, Heb 1:6)**

(303) Without an active faith, you're going to lose ground in every area of your life until you doubt *this Christianity thing*, become stagnant, and drift back into the miserable counterfeits of the world. From the greatest evangelist to the newest convert, ALL are equal in God's eyes—nothing works apart from His word and its outworking grace through you. Just to be saved and then struggle through life isn't the way God planned it. Grow in His living word, live out your faith, and expect great things. You too are destined to save lives!
(Matt 14:31, 21:21, Rom 10:12, James 2:20)

(304) Revitalise your hope: Stop worshiping your problems. Take the spiritual battle to the enemy: spend time learning, thinking about, and praying over the word of God that applies to your own or another's situation and watch God's light roll back the darkness. Three conditions: obediently put God's kingdom before yours, continual repentance, and simply believe that He hears and acts. Nothing happens without activating your faith. God knows your needs, but He reacts to your faith. **(Ps 42:5, 62:5, Lam 3:25, Rom 15:13)**

(305) It took three near-death experiences before God got my attention! Now, I wouldn't want to give up on His love and care for all the riches in the world. Some find Him through the fire of adversity and personal loss; others trip over the cross because of circumstance, sin, alcohol, or drugs. Many simply find His reality early in their lives. One thing though, if you seek Him, you'll find Him. If you cry to him, He will hear and answer you.
(Deut 4:29, 1 Chron 16:11, Ps 34:10, Lam 3:25)

(306) Moses was a prince until he killed a man and spent 40 years in the wilderness herding sheep, but he never gave up on prayer or the promises of God. At the right time, God's time, he led a nation of two million out of bondage. Patient persistent faith through prayer changes you, people, and the world. Your right times will always come, but not because you chose the timing, worried, stamped your feet, or shook an impatient fist . . . they come at the perfect time because you never stopped believing in and communing with God. *'With Him all things are possible.'* **(Num 23:19, Dan 2:0-22, Mark 10:27, James 1:17)**

(307) If your soul is parched by despair, hope is water spilt on sand, and misery and dread overwhelm you. Become a prisoner of hope, not despair. *'Hope deferred makes the heart sick.'* Don't let the past shape your future; there's only today and your tomorrows. A *hope-less* person forever grinds dead seed upon the millstone of their past while the person of vision ploughs new fields of hope, sows them with faith, and never looks back. Cry to God and He'll restore your hope. **(Ps 42:5, 11, 62:5, 23, Prov 13:12, Isa 40:31, Rom 15:13)**

(308) If you think no one cares or loves you today, well Christ does, and He's prepared to love you unconditionally. That's despite whatever you've done in the past, and the blunders and mistakes you're going to make. Check the word of God…nowhere does it say that those who call on His name will be ignored, shunned, punished, condemned or forced to live without forgiveness, hope, and renewal. The peace and joy of the Lord is yours if you want it? That's minute by minute, day by day. Stay close to God and He'll stay close to you. Your fortress isn't within yourself or the world, but in God. See with the eyes of faith and accept His miraculous gift of unconditional love. **(Deut 31:8, Ps 37:24, 55:16, Ps 91)**

(309) Milk or meat: We become *born again,* and we're excited, on fire, and the Holy Spirit performs marvellous things in and through us. Then our flame withers as the world, the flesh, and the devil fight back. Maybe a minister or another Christian hurts us, or we find that we still have problems, and old habits and fears don't want to go. *'In the world you shall have troubles, BUT, be of good cheer, for I have overcome the world.'* **(John 16:33)**

(310) Hope is water to the thirsty, food to the hungry, a lifebelt to the drowning. Hope is the springboard into a fulfilled life. Hope cancels out despair. Hope is a light in the darkness. Hope in the world, others, and our own abilities is no hope at all. Hope is someone bigger than you at the steering wheel of your life. Let go—let God. Hope is the faith to see beyond what we are to what we can be through God's eyes. Become a prisoner of Hope today. **(Ps 33:18, 42:5, Lam 3:25, Rom 15:13, 1 Pet 1:21)**

(311) The secret of our future is hidden in our daily routine, and life only changes when we change our routines. To move on in life, we have to let go of the past and seize the day. We must renew our minds with Holy Spirit power. Instead of constantly reliving our failures, we can change and look forward to what God has for us. His promises of hope are based on His forgiveness and on us letting go of our past. Do not be afraid to live and trust in hope again. The world is full of darkness, but you have the chance to be a light to all. **(Job 33:30, Ps 97:11, Matt 5:16, John 1:5, 2 Cor 4:6)**

(312) The devil knows our weak points, so we need to work on them with the Holy Spirit. Sometimes, like Paul, God allows us to live with a thorn in the flesh, which keeps us close to Him, humble, repentant, and in prayer. We can be ecstatic with God's amazing works one day, but after a week or so we take them all for granted or we forget, and in time, the devil whispers that those acts or events were not of God at all. Stay close to God at all times whatever happens. He mightn't explain everything, but He'll never abandon us. **(2 Cor 12:7)**

(313) *'Tears last for a night but joy comes in the morning.'* Life's full of ups and downs often without logic or human understanding. Don't try and second guess God's ways for they're higher than ours. His reasoning is far beyond ours. He deigns to ride the rollercoaster with us. He cannot forsake us or ever abandon us. He collects our every tear and they rest with Him in a place beside our prayers where Christ now sits, so keep the fire of hope burning bright. **(Ps 30:5, Isa 61:2, Jer 31:16, 2 Cor 1:3)**

(314) Do you need love, understanding, peace, or wisdom? Do you seek healing, answers, somewhere to cast your cares? Do you want a light in the darkness, a safe way? Do you need comforting, rescuing, forgiving? Perhaps your soul needs restoring, your prayer life energising, your faith refuelling? Are these wilderness days when you cannot find hope for your spirit? All your permanent answers are found in Christ, not man, things, or mammon. Turn to God and He will turn your life around.
(Ps 23, John 14:1 *AMP*, 2 Cor 1:8-10)

(315) We often forget God, but He never forgets the covenant He sealed with us; never fails on a promise, and we're often surprised when divine intervention occurs at exactly the right time. He honours every prayer made in His will, yet we fail to keep their importance in mind. He remains faithful when we're not. He rescues from every pit. Stay under his blessing. Seek him today; reaffirm your first love, and dust off His promises to you.
(Gen 9:11-13, Deut 7:9, Neh 9:19, Ps 94:14, 2 Cor 1:20, 2 Pet 3:8-9)

(316) When we stop looking inward at our faults and limitations and start looking outward with hope, we'll always grow, become more Christ-like, do great works, and fulfil our calling. Let the Holy Spirit continue to change you as you give to those who need what God has invested in you. Christian growth is about letting go of self; surrendering earthly desires to gain heaven's riches. The devil wants you stuck in a rut, caught up with yourself, but God wants you free and journeying with Him.
(Ps 73:26, Mark 14:38, Rom 8:4-17, Eph 6:12)

(317) *'The Lord will perfect that which concerns me.'* There are no half measures with God. Once He sees you past the cross, the race to the finish line begins in earnest. *'He who has started a good work in you will bring it to completion.'* The potter concentrates on a lump of clay until he has produced a worthy, beautiful, and useful vessel; each piece designed for a specific purpose. None are rejected, and that includes you! **(Ps 138:8, Phil 1:6)**

(318) Be encouraged, become a prisoner of Hope. Despite our constant mistakes, it's impossible for the God of the second chance not to love, rescue, and accept us. Peter knew such abounding grace after he deserted Jesus. Jesus gladly restored him. Peter went on to do mighty things and fulfil his life's calling. The cross paves the way to constant forgiveness and mercy for the penitent and obedient heart. That's His overcoming love for all of us, especially as we fail so often. **(Ps 42:5 & 11, 62:5, Isa 40:31, Rom 15:13)**

(319) God delights in you. He sings over you. You are His joy, the apple of His eye. He'll give you no bad thing. He's stored up treasures for you. He loves you unconditionally and chooses never to forsake you. He's but a prayer away. He sees Christ in you. He believes in you; has plans for you, old or young. He opens and closes the appropriate doors for your good. He's your bread and breath and reason for being! He is *'I AM'*, and that's all you need to hear, know, and believe by faith!
(Exod 3:14, Deut 32:10, Jer 29:11, Zeph 3:17)

(320) Guarding your hope is like protecting a chick fallen from its nest: you feed it, keep it warm, apply tender love and care, and nurture it until it's ready to fly free. Don't lose the precious promise hope brings. Faith through hope raises the spirit, soothes the soul; she rides the storms, the ordinariness of day, and the long emptiness of night. Hope is ice water to a parched tongue. Never take your eyes off the one who brings hope, Jesus. Let Him restore your soul today. **(Ps 23, 25:5 & 21, 39:3, Rom 12:12, 15:4, 13)**

(321) *'I will deliver my beloved.'* Ever been in a tough spot, sent up an arrow prayer and been delivered? God cares about every breath you take, but until His mission in you is accomplished and He takes you home, you'll live in an imperfect world. That means the devil will ride your back, and you'll make many mistakes, backslide occasionally, and sometimes want to abandon your faith. Call unto God. He loves to deliver and restore; set you back on your feet, so that you can soar like the eagle again. **(Ps 37, Isa 40:31)**

(322) *'I will dwell in God's house forever.'* Part of being in Christ is to know God will welcome you home when you've finished His work here. No more tears, hardship, pain, or suffering. Jesus went ahead and prepared a room for each of us. Many fear death, but we don't need to worry, as faith carries us home in blessed assurance of our place in the Kingdom of Heaven. **(Ps 23, John 14:2)**

(323) Memories of my early life were of being angry, frustrated, and miserable a lot of the time, broken relationships, and an often busted heart. I never got what I hoped for or desired. One such desperate time, God found me in a gutter, stood me up, dusted me down, and said: "I got you, and we're going to work things out. It'll take time, but I'm in the business of changing people permanently, making them whole. Is anything impossible for Me?" Let Him talk to you about your rattling skeletons today. Only He can bury them permanently! **(Matt 19:26, Mark 10:27)**

(324) Who are you in Christ? You've been saved—permanently. Not under judgement but grace. You've eternal life. You've all the power of God through His Holy Spirit thanks to Christ. You're redeemed. You're blessed with God's favour. He directs your paths. You need want for nothing. You live by faith alone. Love, peace, and joy are yours by birthright. You're not an orphan in this world, but a child of the living God. You're a priest and king! Start to live as one who is a brother of Christ and a son of the living God. **(Eph 1:1-23)**

Barrie Kibble

RENEWAL

'Empty containers serve no other purpose than to collect dust
on a shelf.'

(325) When we stop giving time to the word of God our faith dissipates and we're surprised when the amazing things we saw in answer to prayer no longer happen; we wonder where God is? God never went anywhere, but often because of the cares of this world we lose sight of Him. We get a few knocks and we stop and dig in, or we simply stray from the narrow path. God's arms are ever open and He bares no grudges! Confess, renew your walk with Him, get back into His word, and things will start to happen again for your good and the good of others.
(Matt 4:4, Luke 11:28, Acts 20:32, 1 Thess 2:13, Heb 4:12)

(326) If you're fed up being locked into the same old ruts and sins, then you have to allow the Holy Spirit to *'renew your mind.'* This miracle starts with confession and reading and declaring God's word over your life, then you can form new thought patterns and develop true character that can't be crushed by the storms of life. Surrender the old patterns, yes, but you have to work with the Spirit and the Word to achieve permanent change—it's not automatic.
(Rom 12:2)

(327) God always answers the doorbell! Has your Christian walk become hopeless, have your dreams been shattered, has misery, hurt, and fear overwhelmed you? Let God restore your soul and renew your walk of faith. Meditate on God's word for your peace of mind and rekindled hope. Stop letting the enemy take previously hard-fought ground from you through fear, sickness, hardship, sin, or faltering faith. Remember: *'Faith comes by hearing, and hearing by the word of God.'* **(Ps 23, Prov 2:5-8, Rom 10:17)**

(328) Have you messed up? Shock horror—we all do, continually! Christ understands; that's why He walked this earth, suffered as we do, and even laid down His life for us although He never messed up. In death He overcame hell, regained His majesty in heaven, and made room for each of us there—made a way to God; got rid of every blockage between us and Him. *'Seek the Lord while He may be found; call on Him while He is near.' 'Let the wicked forsake his way and his evil thoughts. Let him turn to God and He will have mercy on him.'* He freely pardons and rebuilds, always doing a new thing for your good. **(Isa 55:6-7, 1 John 1:9)**

(329) Failing faith: All who accept Christ and then fall, for whatever reason, have no need to look back in anger or question His presence. The true and living God brings life to dead tissue and dry bones through His Holy Spirit. Seek Him now and He *will* be found. Let Him restore and breathe life back into that which seems dead. God's been too busy loving you, understanding you, and weeping with you to have deserted you; of all people, His son knows how tough the Christian life is; that's why the real rewards are stored up in Heaven for you. He knows you couldn't handle them on this fallen earth just like Adam and Eve. **(Ezek 37:3-5)**

(330) Paying the price 1: To fear God is to worship Him in Holy Spirit and truth—to hate and flee from sin; to adhere to and carry out all His commands and precepts. Do you wonder why your ministry is not blossoming, peace and joy are fleeting, and prayer goes answered? The fear of God is the beginning of wisdom; wisdom is the word of God, and His word is His will. *'If you ask anything according to His will you have it.'* Don't expect anything if sin and worldly or self-worship are your standard. Hate sin and worship God; know and act on His will and heaven's warehouses open their doors. **(1 John 5:14)**

(331) Paying the price 2: The day I decided to totally trust and obey God and do whatever He said, even if I lost everything like Job, was the day God turned my life around. Now I need for nothing. I don't know what tomorrow or next week will bring, but I'm a prisoner of hope, and I trust God implicitly because I have proved He *is* faithful to His word. I simply did what He asked. I already had a holy fear (awe/deep respect) of Him and I decided to trust to His word without conditions. There are no short cuts—do what God asks and everything in your life will fit into place. **(Zech 9:12, Luke 11:28, Phil 4:6-7)**

(332) Whether you live in fear and misery or peace and joy is your choice. God has fulfilled His part of the eternal covenant with you through Christ. Life here and now is about renewing your mind, staying in faith, and saving the lost. The mind can be reprogrammed if you are willing to try. Hard at first, but it does get easier. *'Faith comes by hearing.'* If you don't read the word, your faith flounders and nothing changes. You'll always be panic-calling to God instead of praying calmly with an expectant faith. Finally, you need to trust fully in His answer when it comes, receive and act on it—whatever that may be. **(Rom 10:17, 12:2)**

(333) *'He restores my soul.'* People and circumstance wear us down. We become anxious, exhausted, damaged by words or deeds, or our own failings and irrational fears; hope dies, trust withers, faith stumbles, and the Jesus-vision blurs. We lose our grip on God's promises which are vital to a healthy soul. The good shepherd listens out for the desperate cries of his sheep, wounded, ensnared or lost, and He gladly rescues them. Look to the cross, repent if needs be, and call on Him now. **(Ps 23, Jer 29:11-14)**

(334) To be a Christian and make a positive impact on people and situations, you have to stand up and be counted—it's guaranteed to cost you, but God's honour and rewards far outweigh fleshy, earthly loss. Don't take my word for it, *'Taste and see that the Lord is good.'* **(Ps 34:8, Luke 9:23-25)**

PERSEVERANCE
'A flag planted atop a mountain is seen clearer than one planted midway.'

(335) We can rarely undo our mistakes and bad decisions, but God, through His Son, has made room for all our failures. The ashes of hurts, selfishness, broken promises, damaged relationships, lost loves and sorrows shall fade. We must keep picking up the cross, stick at this new journey. We'll fall, but He'll always rescue. At days end, we'll stand firm on the rock if we don't give up on His hope seeded in us. Our success is dependant on God, not people or events from the past. **(Josh 1:8, Ps 30:6-7, Phil 3:13-14)**

(336) The devil has a ravenous appetite! His prime concern is to keep us from God. Foolish converts are meat for misery if they think becoming a Christian is a safe back-pocket ticket to heaven. It's a lifelong spiritual battle that starts the day we came to Christ. Boot camp has to end. In order to grow, God sends us into the world, the wilderness of life, but He equips us with everything we need to overcome. We must act with faith if we want to grow and see victory over our flesh, the world, and the devil.
(Deut 20:4, Ps 20:6, 2 Tim 3:16-17, 1 John 5:4)

(337) Our principles and morals are often hard won. They're fashioned from parent and circumstance, from our walk with God, and from those we consider upright and true, honest and courageous, passionate and merciful. Christ stuck with His God-given mission and never sold out to the world or the devil. We need to follow His example or life becomes meaningless, and we'll find it hard to live with ourselves and others with us.
(Ps 25:21, Prov 10:9, 1 Cor 15:33, Phil 4:8, Titus 2:7)

(338) If you can't look back and see what God has done in your life then you'll not look forward in faith for more and greater miracles. God's always doing something new and always for your best. Meditate on the times He's rescued you, blessed you, answered prayer, and stretched you. Remember the day He called you and you gave your days to Him. Before you step out again, do it with confidence, for the Lord is ever with you.
(Josh 4:4-8, Ps 18:16-18, 2 Pet 3:2)

(339) Christian Soldiers: God always moves forward and expands His kingdom through us on earth; we're His *salvation army*. He wants us on the frontline with Him, not bringing up the rear all the time. Rest and recuperation are important, and sometimes we are wounded, but we mustn't loiter in the field hospital, the canteen, or the supply tents. We're called to be in the vanguard and share in Christ's victorious, overcoming life: **(1 Tim 6:12, 2 Tim 4:7)**

(340) As Christians, three things will always trip us up and make us useless and miserable: The world, the flesh, and the devil. If you're not vigilant, you'll be taken out by one of them, or a combination of all three. Do you recognise the voice of God through all the static of life warning you of traps and snares? If not, you don't have a close enough relationship with Him or you're in sin and out of His blessing, and you'll continue to fall foul to the three enemies of your soul. Stay close to God, and you'll dwell in peace despite every circumstance. **(Ps 91)**

(341) Agreement with God motivates purpose and passion, bestows favour on all you do, and is a friend of obedience. Often, it's hard to act on what God asks because it seems crazy in the eyes of others. King David danced through the streets of Jerusalem to praise God, and those that despised him were cursed. Don't worry what people think, leave them to God. Just do what God asks, and you'll bring light into darkness, water into deserts, life into death. **(Deut 28:1, 1 Kings 2:3, Ps 128:1, 2 John 1:6)**

(342) Jesus is still God's plan A. Flood or no flood, there was never ever a plan B. It's the same with your life hidden with Him; He's moulding and crafting you to fulfil your part in plan A, so you can get the best out of life and heaven. That's what unflinching love costs, heavenly majesty put aside for flesh and blood as a sacrifice for sin; Christ instead of you; grace instead of judgement, forgiveness instead of a reckoning, and life instead of death. Try to comprehend today the truth of who you are in Christ, your freedom, and the power you contain as a child of God full of the Holy Spirit. **(Rom 5:8, 6:4, 8:11, 8:38-39, Eph 1, Col 4:17)**

(343) Success in kingdom matters isn't measured by money or the material, but how far you've grown and travelled with God through obedience. Growth is a reflection of what's happened to others because of you and how much you've changed to become more like Christ. The world already has its reward, but all yours are kept safe in heaven where rust, fire, creditors, and thieves cannot take them from you. Run the race well. Put others before self, and God will raise you up at the right time.
(Gen 15:1, 2 Sam 22:25, 2 Chron 15:7, Ps 19, Matt 5:12, Heb 11:6)

(344) Just as winter leads to spring and summer to autumn, there are seasons in your life too. The right time for things to happen according to God's will—not too early, never too late. The farmer plants his crop and gets on with life. He's not anxious, as he knows the crop will be ready at the right time. Learn to wait with patient faith, for God's word bears fruit at precisely the right time if you don't keep digging up your seed to see if it's growing (doubt). Trust God to bring you through everything, and to fulfil all His promises at their appointed time. Reaffirm your trust in specific prayers today and rebuild your faith—you might waver, but God never does. **(Gen 26:12, Eccles 3:1-8, 11:4, James 5:7)**

(345) Are you feeling miserable, downcast, fearful, full of dread or confused? God hasn't left; you just need to re-tune your soul. Ask God to restore your soul (mind, will, and emotions) to its default settings in heaven. You can give up on God, but the devil will never stop hounding you. There's nothing more God needs to do thanks to Christ. Trust all to God and speak His word—take Christ's authority over your feelings. **(Ps 23, Luke 10:18-20, Col 2:10)**

(346) Patience: People's souls are God's business. He chooses when, where, and how to save them. You may be in a long line of witnesses before God's word opens the heart of a person. One plants, another waters, but the Holy Spirit causes growth and reaps the harvest. Keep praying and trusting God for friends and family, colleagues, and strangers. I have many Christian friends and two saved cousins to prove perseverance pays. Let go, let God.
(1 Cor 3:6, Col 3:12, Heb 6:12)

(347) *'The valley of the death-shadow.'* All of us will suffer tough times. What matters is how we endure them and who with. If we didn't have bad days, we'd never see the value in the good ones. No, it's not easy to persevere through trials, but we're not of those who give up but of those who run the race despite sickness, heartache, and loss. Sheep fall ill, are hurt or often fearful, and some die, but if they belong to the Good Shepherd, He never leaves their side. A few of us must watch friends or relatives pass through the greatest valley, and they'll need our strength, support, prayers, and above all, our unfailing love. **(Ps 23, Heb 12:1, James 1:3)**

(348) What challenges face you in the days ahead? Need a new job? Want to repair a broken relationship? Sort your finances? Fight or cope with illness? In which area of your life do you need peace, resolution, healing, or victory? *'With God nothing is impossible,'* so start oiling your FAITH through prayer; get the engine of HOPE running; TRUST Him to map the perfect route. If you don't start the engine, you're not going to move the car. **(Mark 10:27, James 2:26)**

(349) Life passes faster than a camera flash. Where have you placed your investments: in people, the material? Will you be remembered? Did you affect people's lives for the good or did you bury your talents? Did you make the most of every opportunity or were you afraid to make mistakes? Fearlessly do what God and your heart tells you to do. Don't forsake the Lord for He will not forsake you, for His investment is His kingdom in you. Your reward is eternal life with Him. **(John 5:24, 17:3, Gal 6:8)**

(350) What mountains are you facing today? Is your confidence in self and the material, or in God? He doesn't always deliver an obvious and spectacular sign such as parting the Red Sea, but you do have His word and His promises. You need to search for, learn, and live out those promises applicable to you; quantify, accept, and apply them by faith. *'Call into being the things that are not as if they were.'* **(Rom 4:17)**

(351) *'The Lord is your rock, your fortress, and your deliverer in whom you can take refuge'* whatever your circumstances. Let Him be your shield and saviour. *'Draw close to Him and He will draw close to you.'* Don't let another moment pass until you've talked with Him, shared all your cares, and praised him despite your situation whether good or bad. Even if you don't understand the why and what of things, trust Him. Stand firm! Let nothing shake your resolve and faith today. **(2 Sam 22:2, Ps 18:2, 62:6, James 4:8)**

(352) Learning faith by degrees: David had to kill the bear and lion before he had the faith to kill Goliath. Are you running ahead of God's grace and provision and hitting a brick wall, running out of hope and spiritual joy? Is your Goliath winning; has he stripped you of your sling and stones? Do you continually fail and end up with withering faith and nagging doubt? Maybe you want to be a king before you've been a servant, or to instantly level mountains when you can't even remove a pimple? The Father says, "Build your house on rock not sand—one brick of faith at a time." Start small but dream big. **(Jude 1:20)**

WITNESS
'People only know what they've seen or heard for
themselves.'

(353) We're not called to save ourselves but the lost. Whatever your circumstances, if you want to be filled by God's amazing blessings of peace, joy and completeness pressed down and overflowing, you need to empty yourself into others. Give them what He's given you. The time of greatest joy in your life is when you sacrifice yourself for others. Jesus said, *"For your joy to be full I hung on a cross."* To non-believers walking in the flesh, that's a peculiar statement, but to the saved that walk in the Spirit of God, it makes perfect sense—so go tell the lost what you have for them. **(Phil 2:3, Heb 12:2)**

(354) Mind-boggling to the proud and utterly foolish to the ignorant: God chooses to work out His kingdom through those He calls sons and daughters. We are adopted into the Holy Trinity of God-Jesus-Spirit. No, I can't explain this, nor do I want or need to. I simply believe it because it works—it can work for anyone who simply believes. Christ lives in those who accept Him, and power is through the baptism of the Holy Spirit, without whom we are powerless as Christians. If He lives in us, then we have all the attributes of the Son and can do what Jesus did. All this on earth and everlasting life too!
(Matt 21:22, Mark 5:36, 9:23, Rom 10:11, Eph 1:18-20, Phil 2:12)

(355) When you witness Christ, don't water down the message through fear, nor exaggerate your experiences to convince people of its truth. It's not your job to help people find Christ, but the Holy Spirit's. So relax, be yourself, speak the truth of your experience whether you're young or old in the faith. Don't fuss when you're rejected; dust yourself off, and pray for the next chance. **(Matt 10:16, Mark 6:11, Acts 1:8)**

(356) Dismiss the idea if we will, but one day everyone will have to give account for the life God gave them. If you didn't accept Christ, then excuses about thinking it was a nice story or you being a good person won't keep you from eternal separation from God. To those who accepted Christ and were forgiven and changed there's no judgment, only a spiritual body and an eternal crown, but those who reject Christ will have to give full account for every sin, and then pay for them all eternally. **(Matt 12:36, Rom 2:5, 2 Cor 5:10)**

(357) Finding God 1: Trusting in a living God in this modern age is hard, yet people are willing to seek answers to life's problems in tarot cards, fortune tellers, cults, and other con-trick-candy of the devil. Like rabid dogs, these dark arts eventually turn and tear mind and body apart, filling them with hell on earth. God's always calling to those who find it hard to trust His love and care in a world of sudden death, loss, and misery. Call Him back. He earnestly desires to talk with you. **(Hab 2:18, Acts 17:22-24)**

(358) Finding God 2: Failed relationships because we trusted fully in them instead of God can be difficult if not impossible to repair. When God starts a relationship, He's in it with you to the end of days and into heaven. Based on unconditional love and continuing forgiveness, all those who seek God and accept Christ as Lord will find permanence to everything wholesome in their life that has always escaped them. **(Job 8:5-6, Rom 8:39, Heb 11:6)**

(359) Finding God 3: To forgive isn't easy and often impossible without God fighting your corner. When we forgive the hurts done by others we ourselves are healed of crippling physical and mental scars. Christ said, *'Come unto me all you who are heavy laden and I will give rest.'* Without a God-relationship some will never be able to forgive others, God, and themselves, nor ever see good reason to do so. **(Matt 11:28, 18:21-35)**

(360) Finding God 4: No kind act, thought suppression, lie, pretence, drug, or drink can ever remove the debilitating power and misery of guilt. One of the fantastic and humbling gifts of knowing and walking with God is peace; it's a total peace that passes all human understanding. Christ nailed guilt to the cross so that we can be free to live the way God planned, in harmony with ourselves and others with complete peace of mind. **(Rom 15:13, Phil 4:6-9)**

(361) Finding God 5: Only God can forgive sin. Sin is rejecting Christ and living however you please; refusing to recognise a loving God. You may have lied, thieved, cheated, sowed lust and hatred, been full of anger, played with the occult, or simply lived life saying, "to hell with God and everyone else." Let Father God break those chains and give you the perfect life He's planned for you. Redemption is never too late.
(Num 14:18, Isa 59:1, 1 Cor 1:30, Eph 1:7)

(362) If you find belief in a Father God stupid, you'll find life pointless after trying everything else. If you find it laughable that a God would give up His Son for you to be forgiven, you'll find the last laugh is on you. If miracles aren't for you, then you'll lose hope in reality. If you think becoming one of God's elect is foolishness, you hand the devil the keys to your life. So don't blame God when the world, the flesh, and the devil regularly mess you up. God longs to know you and love you.
(Ps 42:7-8, Isa 12:3, 30:15, 58:11, 65:1, Jer 17:7-8)

(363) Prove God: Jesus caught people's attention with the truth about themselves through miracles of healing and deliverance from demons. People followed him everywhere simply because of these amazing acts. All those He touched experienced His unconditional love and received His message of deliverance from sickness, healed of mental and physical disorders, sin expunged forever. He met all their needs and He can meet yours. Yet many rejected Him and still do. Who do you follow?
(Deut 31:6, Matt 16:24, John 3:36, 8:12, 12:26, 1 Thess 4:8)

(364) There are three amazing facets of the heavenly realm that believe in your salvation, God the father, Jesus the son, and their Holy Spirit. The only way for God to become flesh and save us from ourselves was to sacrifice one facet, Christ the son, to release another, the Holy Spirit. Yet all three are one! That's mind-boggling? It's not for us to reason the Trinity with our limited comprehension, but simply believe with big hearts.
(Gen 1:1, Matt 4:17, Rev 12:10)

(365) If we can't say sorry to God for the way we've lived and accept Christ at the helm, life will remain haphazard, often miserable and meaningless. We marvel at this planet, outer space, and our own being, yet still cannot accept a supreme creator. We give into the worst of our traits: Rebellion. There'll be no excuses before the face of God when we die, for He offered His son and everything else besides so we could live an overcoming life without regret. Seek God today and you will find Him.
(Isa 1:5, 55:1, Matt 6:33, John 4:12-14, Heb 3:7-9)

(366) The devil's biggest lie: "Life is all about you and your happiness." This is the perfect formula for countless failures, disappointments, and miseries. God's gift to live in freedom and a full life is through Christ. People only know true joy when they set Jesus in first place and put others before themselves. Many don't like that, as it means letting go, being transparent, and surrendering to a greater power than them.
(John 8:44, Eph 4:27, Heb 2:14, James 4:7, 1 John 3:8)

(367) Ninety-percent of people I meet believe in some sort of *Supreme Being*. They also believe in prayer when everything goes wrong; they suddenly recognise their lives are mostly miserable, powerless, their hopes uncertain, and that death is final. I tell them the God they are seeking is the Father of Jesus Christ. He's pure Spirit fashioned of pure LOVE, and He's all around them and hears their prayers, but due to unbelief in His grace through the cross, they've rendered Him impotent to act. They've rejected His reality and truths. I also tell them the way to freedom because God wants to wipe the slate clean, pour His Holy Spirit into them, *'Give them a hope and a future,'* and let them fulfil His purposes for a life well-lived and enjoyed with value, peace, faith, and hope. **(Jer 8:9, 29:11, 1 John 4:15)**

(368) There are souls who dread life; cannot wait to see the back of it. They drown in unforgivingness or painful memories, loneliness, depression, stress, dread and anxiety; racked with fear or guilt, or numbed by loss. Poverty and hunger lurk at doors, and a desperate few grope for a reason to go on. We need to be open to their needs and not count the cost; get rid of the world's tinsel that masks Christ's birth, death, and resurrection, and reach out to people. You might be the only light they see in their darkness. Christ is the beacon of hope, so keep that torch burning! **(Matt 5:16, 10:8, Rom 5:5)**

(369) There's no short cut to a meaningful life. Without God at the wheel, everything you do or hope for will end in dissatisfaction, dead ends, and disappointments, or at least unfulfilled potential, wasted talents, and your *'pearls cast before swine.'* You only have to look at the wonders of creation to know there's a God and a heaven; you only have to look at godless people and the misery in this world to know there's a devil and a hell. Take the narrow path with Christ and fulfil your God-given potential.
(Matt 7:6 & 13-14, Gal 5:7, Heb 12:1)

(370) If you trust in idols, in karma, hopping on one leg for a day, giving to charity to expunge your conscience, yoga, *feng shui*, horoscopes or things made of wood, plastic or iron, best realize that none of them are alive; none of them can save your soul or give you a life worth living; none of them can comfort, change or speak to you, and none of them can restore, forgive and empower you to give and receive love—only God can do that. Don't leave it too late before you decide to get to know the living God and throw out all your dead gods.
(Lev 26:1, Josh 24:15, Ps 42:2, John 4:10)

(371) Unlike the Holy Spirit, the devil can't be everywhere at once, hence his legions of demons. He's the father of lies, spiritual deception, division among the elect, and fear; the more people that go to hell the better, especially those who mock any perception of God or hell, and those who label themselves Christians but don't accept Christ or tread the godly life. Pray for the lost that the scales fall from their eyes. **(Luke 10:19, Col 2:15, 1 John 5:4)**

(372) The lost: Sin's plague is eternal separation from the God of love. Pray fervently, without ceasing for those who don't know Christ; never give up on them—family, friends, and strangers all matter, so hold fast to prayer. The lost are cynical of hell's nightmare and try to make the best of life, yet their judgement will be a dreadful matter. The cross, the nails, the acute suffering are love personified for them—so is the resurrection, that no one else need perish. Persevere in prayer for the lost.
(Mark 16:15, Rom 6:23, Eph 6:18)

(373) Sow good seed: Conversion is seldom instant. Many may be involved in that journey for a single soul. Be yourself and stick to your unadulterated faith; no exaggerations, impatience or defensive posturing. Jesus, not men, saves through the Holy Spirit. Christ wants lovers of people not zealots of religion, gardeners not undertakers. The blood of the lamb and the witness of your testimony are both seed and crop growth, but God chooses the moment of harvest. **(Isa 55:11, 1 Cor 3:6, Rev 12:11)**

(374) Collateral damage: When we gossip or curse, refuse to forgive or continue in sin, we expand the boundaries of darkness both in ourselves and this world; God's power through us shrinks and our light dims, our witness fades. Don't quench the Spirit nor dampen the flames of integrity, truth, faith, and hope. Make a positive difference, and be a constant reflection of Christ to the lost, or they could remain lost. Non Christians are watching us to see if we live what we believe—so is God. **(Phil 2:1-15, Col 4:5)**

(375) Many think we're annoying Bible-bashers, hoodwinked, freaks with our heads in the clouds. We don't argue or defend ourselves; we only speak the truth of what happened when Christ hit home, and God made a way for Himself and man to meet again. Many believe God's dead. We know He's alive and kicking. We don't have all the answers to tragedy, natural disaster, war, etc; but we're not supposed to. Let go, let God. Be honest, the world is a mess because the proud and rebellious demand they go it alone and insist on taking us with them. That isn't what God planned, but you don't need to miss His plan for you! Keep Bible-bashing, it saves lives. **(2 Cor 12:19)**

(376) The Lord's work: Afraid to speak or wondering how to? God only needs you in the right place at the right time. In ordinary moments or divine appointments, just be yourself. Many mock the truth. Let it go; they're God's problem. Above all, it's God's work, so be quick to listen and slow to speak; give the Holy Spirit elbow room. Keep casting your testimony, and in due time the fish will bite heaven's bait. **(Acts 4:29, 28:31, Rev 12:11)**

(377) God or self: Non Christians are drawn to the living God when we reflect Christ, instead of us tyre-levering our own formulas to answer their hurts and needs. Often, we go about witnessing like ignorant children pulling the tail of a bone-chewing Rottweiler. If we can't reflect the love and compassion of Christ, the lost only experience us, not God. We're light and salt—ambassadors for Christ, not for self. **(Matt 5:13-16, 2 Cor 3:3, Eph 4:1, 1 Pet 3:15)**

(378) *'For You are with me.'* Is your god the LIVING God? Can He change you or the lives of others through you? Can worshiping the material, the inanimate, save souls? Will mantras, sacred cows, religious effigies, elephant gods, and trying to be good save us? Life is our living spirit meeting God's living Holy Spirit, not a fickle union with flesh, plastic, metal, wood, or stone. Sheep know when their good shepherd is close because they hear his voice. **(Ps 23, Acts 17:23)**

(379) To be you, warts and all, is tough, and you'll find a lot of people won't like you unless you conform to their moulds. God forever calls to you in spirit and soul. The quicker your barriers crumble, the faster He can change you to be like Christ; live a full life free to bless others. Many say He doesn't exist, that doesn't mean He doesn't. Instead of listening to the naysayers, search for yourself. Why resist a Father of grace, or abandon the thought of a saviour, when we cry from within to be accepted and saved by more than our own flesh? Talk to God today. **(1 Cor 2:2, 2 Cor 10:12)**

Barrie Kibble

THE HOLY SPIRIT
'God's holy power works in us so we can emulate Jesus.'

(380) Preaching or witnessing without Holy Spirit power is futile, like sweeping leaves in a gale. Without the supernatural, God's word is well-meant but powerless. Seek the Spirit and manifestations of Him through miraculous words, gifts, signs and wonders—not for show or sensation, but for God to validate the power and glory of His word. The Spirit was *sealed* in you as a sign when you were saved. Without Him, the Christian walk is a long, dreary trudge uphill; you'll preach or witness in the flesh and it'll change nothing, neither move you or others a single inch forward. Listen to His Spirit. **(Acts 1:8, 10:38, Rom 15:13, 1 Thess 1:5)**

(381) *'You anoint my head with oil.'* Ancient priests and kings know this honour, the oil that seals a calling. That blessed mark of ownership; the seal of unconditional love and acceptance poured out by the Holy Spirit on sons and daughters of the living God. We're kings and priests! The good shepherd applies salve to his sheep for healing, oil to keep pests from ears and eyes; sheep recognize the fragrance, eager for more. **(Ps 23)**

(382) There's nothing weak or boring about being a Christian unless you don't believe in the manifestations of the Holy Spirit. God's power is manifested though His Spirit. Faith is made real and active through His Spirit. No true conversion, no healing or miracle is possible because Christianity is powerless without Him. We cannot change and demons cannot be delivered without the Spirit. He's God's power in action on earth through Christ.
(Acts 1:8, 5:32, 8:15-16, 15:8, 19:1-4)

(383) Don't avoid or despise the Holy Spirit; you can do nothing in God without Him. Surrendering to any other belief, hope, system or person is foolish. Many feel safe with a rote prayer list or a good old sing song on a Sunday, or try to act holy. But there's no power in anything we do in His name without the Holy Spirit shaking and shaping us. Believers live and are led by Him, and we worship in Spirit and in truth, or at best it is a fleshy, powerless dirge. Seek God's Spirit today. **(John 14:26, Acts 1:8, 4:31, 10:38, 15:8, Eph 1:13)**

(384) You can't be an effective Christian in its working-out-reality without recognising and accepting the Holy Spirit. Refuse or ignore the power of the Spirit, and Godly living and doing is like pushing a dead elephant uphill. You're sealed with His Spirit at salvation, but you need to release His power in your life every day: *'Not by (our) might nor by (our) power, but by God's Spirit.'* He's waiting to empower you! **(Zech 4:6)**

(385) Drink of Christ and you'll never be thirsty. In fact, what He pours out will bless you and overflow into others. If you're in Christ and your cup is not running over, check where your bucket's at. Is it on the lip, halfway down, or did you forget to pull it up? Live like Christ and emulate His character and works. He is the water, the wellspring of life, and you need Him. Others need Him too, especially those who are dying of thirst. To reflect Christ, you must live and act like Him, draw and learn from Him—let the Holy Spirit have free reign with you. **(Isa 44:3, 55:1, John 4:14)**

(386) *"Beloved, you can do nothing without My Spirit working in you, through you. He is the gateway to life in abundance; the mark of the cross in your spirit, and the mind of Christ in your ways. Welcome Him with open arms, and He'll be your advocate, friend, captain, helper, and comforter. He'll lead you into all truth."* **(John 14:26, 16:13, Acts 1:8, 4:31, 1 Pet 1:12)**

(387) The Spirit flows like a river. Ask and He drenches you. God doesn't keep good gifts from his beloved, but pours them out freely. We need to get off the river bank and into the water—ankle deep, knee deep, deep enough to swim. The Spirit turns weakness to strength, hearts of stone to flesh, despair to hope, double-mindedness to action, self-consciousness to God-consciousness, and death into life. **(Ps 46:4, Ezek 47:1-12, Rev 22:1)**

(388) Keep a healthy spiritual balance; don't just seek the gifts but the giver, God. The Spirit enables certain gifts at certain times. However, we all have one inbuilt gift that works alongside our natural talent. I cannot play a bassoon, but I can write; healing is not my strong suite but prophecy is. The Spirit will help you expand your talents and gifts, so don't be afraid of making mistakes along the way. **(1 Cor 12)**

(389) Getting closer to God is through the Holy Spirit. Prayer, worship, praise, relationships, and word-study can be set ablaze by the Spirit. But empty religion, false piety, spiritual pride, and outright sin grieve the Holy Spirit. He'll quickly withdraw, the blessings dry up, and life and church get tough. God isn't mocked and Christ paid the ultimate price for our sin. Honour their Spirit. **(Isa 63:10, Matt 3:11, John 4:23, Acts 2:3, Eph 4:30)**

(390) Keep on being filled: You fill up with the Spirit and you pour out; it's an ongoing process. He can't refill a vessel that's not emptied for others. Don't let blessings go stale—you can't re-use them! You can do the same works that Jesus did and beyond when you are obedient to God…right place, right time, right situation, and the blessings flow. *'Obedience is better than sacrifice.'*
(1 Sam 15:22, Luke 6:38, John 14:12)

(391) Continually seek God's Spirit and He'll direct your paths, light up God's will, and give you Christ-like thoughts. He'll smooth the bumps, bridge the rivers and ravines, and fill in the potholes; He'll tell you to wait, go back, or go another way. The first principle is to worship God, the second to listen, the third to act, the fourth to praise—in every decision seek the mind of Christ through His Spirit. **(Prov 3:6, Heb 12:12-14)**

(392) You can stick a plug in a socket but unless you flip the switch the power doesn't flow, and nothing's going to work. When you engage with, surrender control to, and embrace the Holy Spirit you're charged with the power to change yourself and those around you. The Spirit does God's work for His glory and you get blessed as a bonus. Shed God's light into areas of darkness in situations and lives by letting the Spirit empower, lead, heal, comfort, convict, save, and teach. **(Eph 6:10, Rom 1:16** *AMP***)**

(393) Who formed the universe, you in the womb, the day you were saved? Who empowers you to walk in Christ, changes lives and situations for good and to God's glory? From Genesis to Revelation, God's Spirit is the power source. God, Christ, Spirit— inseparable! When Christ left, the Holy Spirit came. The very Spirit that empowered Christ can empower us. Even Christ couldn't function without the Holy Spirit. **(Gen 1, Matt 4:1-11)**

(394) "Crying out, shaking, tongues, uncontrolled laughter, sudden tears, dancing, deliverance, the laying on of hands, that's not for me!" Then Kingdom living is going to be a hard, powerless slog. We have ineffective church services, dwindling congregations held together by charity binges, praise without passion, and worship without truth; barren witnessing, joy squandered, risk-less faith, hope sealed in a box, Bibles collecting dust. The Spirit is the supernatural life and power of God. What He can do and the way He does it is for the spiritual realm and not for the flesh! If we want the life-changing, world changing power of the Spirit, we have to get rid of fear and let Him have all of us! **(Mark 14:38, Rom 7:6)**

(395) The great lie of a stagnant church: "By all means pay lip service to the Holy Ghost because He's mentioned in God's word, but don't upset the *status quo*—we do things our way, always have." God's truth is: Who would receive the power of God, a life-saving, life-altering gift from a loving friend and then lock it away, fearful it might change or embarrass them. Such folk miss the essence of a Godly life packed with unlimited divine power. **(Matt 15:11-13, 16:12, 23:13 & 27)**

Barrie Kibble

SERVANTS and LEADERS

'Without a teachable spirit no one can ever be the master of themselves, and never the captain of others.'

(396) If you want be a leader, you're going to have to be a servant. Bible College doesn't make you a leader; it simply means you've acquired more knowledge, which can be just as fatal as none at all! King David knew this only too well. Helping others to walk and run is fine as long as you've served a servant's apprenticeship, know how to wash feet and collect coats. Apprentices learn from their mistakes so they don't pass them on to others. Who have you hurt or mislead lately? Best go put it right, as their future and yours may depend on your humility. **(Prov 16:18, 1 Cor 4:6, 2 Tim 2:15)**

(397) While Christ calls us all as ministers, we need someone at the head with the call and anointing of shepherd. Leaders assume a tremendous responsibility and will be called to greater account for their conduct. Their job is difficult enough without us causing them grief or gossiping about them. If you don't like something they say or do, then confront in love, but be careful, as God might want to change you! Remember, *'God abhors one who sows discord among the brethren.'* Best get that plank out of your eye before you remove another's splinter. **(Prov 6:16-19, 1 Cor 1:10, Heb 13:17)**

(398) Attributes of the Godly shepherd 1: They put your needs and ambitions before their own. They recognise and encourage your calling and gifts. They admit their failings and are open to criticism. They don't punish, threaten, censure, or cut you off. They raise Christ's banner and not their denomination's. They overflow with selfless love, compassion, and justice. They accept where you are at. They don't consider age a stumbling block. **(1 Thess 5:12)**

(399) Attributes of the Godly shepherd 2: They consider you an equal in Christ. They do nothing out of selfish ambition. The Holy Spirit and not a ministry diploma is their confidence and guide: Knowledge puffs up, but understanding and wisdom are self-evident of God's love in their lives. They help you walk the narrow path, and gently guide, not shove or deal harshly with you. They warn of pitfalls, either based on their own experience or told to them by the Holy Spirit. They encourage you to weigh the word of God with their own advice. They encourage individuality in thought and character. Beware those who wish to control you; it's a spirit, but it's not the Holy Spirit. **(Matt 7:15, Heb 13:7)**

(400) Attributes of the Godly shepherd 3: They stand by you whatever happens. They recognise and support your calling, not smother it because it clashes with their ambitions. Their words are chosen with love and they live by Christ's example. They don't seduce, groom, or mislead with falsehoods or hidden agendas nor label their deceit as Godly. They shouldn't be self-deceived into believing that they alone hold the keys to justice or to solely have God's ear on any given matter. Beware those who are wilfully right; convinced they know what is best for you when God's Spirit and your spirit are equally at odds with whatever spirit drives them. **(Heb 13:17, 2 Pet 2:1)**

(401) Attributes of the Godly Shepherd 4: They're the first to forgive and the last to judge. They understand your mistakes, pick you up, dust you off, and set you back on the right path. They're beside you when you hurt, grieve, are sick or confused, or fat with sin. They gently steer not ride roughshod. They listen to and respect those with experience. They never misuse the word of God. Their sermons are empowered by the Holy Spirit and not the flesh. The Spirit brings conviction, wisdom, gifting, healing, deliverance, revelation, and above all . . . good fruit. Be alert, for by their fruit you shall know flesh from Spirit. **(1 Tim 5:17, Matt 7:16, 20)**

(402) Teacher or disciple, when you've made a mistake, don't plough on and make things worse by not accepting it due to embarrassment, fear, insecurity, or pride. Apologise, make restitution if you can, then you're free to move forward again. Nothing's chiselled in stone apart from the day you were born and the day you die. Stubbornness, belligerence, or a failure to admit you are wrong muzzles life. Your bad decisions hurt and damage others, but above all you; they stunt your growth and hamstring your joy and peace. **(James 5:16)**

(403) Milk or meat: Without prayer and God's blessing we throw ourselves into *this* ministry and *that* mission, and that becomes our all. Then our good works flounder, people change, things end, and we are left high and dry, angry with God. God says this Kingdom stuff is not all about you. If you want to lead, you must become a servant. Stick purely to the WORD and prayer, and God will sort out everything else. **(Ps 127:1, Mark 9:35)**

(404) *'Iron sharpens iron.'* A spirit of unity builds a Christ-like-life. Teamwork is essential, pooling our gifts and abilities. People of faith inspire others to faith. Encouragement is the catalyst; to listen more important than to talk. Consensus on a God-plan is health to the individual and the church. Spiritual safety lies under the umbrella of accountability. There are many traps and predators to snare lone wolves. Accept the wisdom, guidance, and authority of your peers and leaders, and stay on track. **(Prov 27:17)**

(405) The absolute power of God's word: Many suffer from illness, depression, etc; we've prayed and been prayed for until the cows come home, yet nothing ever changes? That's not God's plan—it's the devil's! We can't deny that what we have is 'fact' because it's real, but when *we decide* to refuse to accept that 'fact' and start to declare 'truth' we are set free! Only 'everlasting truth' can change 'temporal fact'. God's settled everything in Heaven for us through Christ, but we must make a stand in that 'truth'; we must think and speak God's word over 'fact' until 'truth' breaks its miserable back! We must believe and speak nothing else, either to ourselves or to others, or we continue to accept 'the fact' and deny 'the truth' and so remain in bondage. **(Isaiah 53:5) (John14:6) (Eph Ch1) (1 Peter 2:24)**

Is God speaking to you but you don't know Him?

If you've picked up or purchased this book and you don't know the living God, maybe you sense it's time you did. Knowing God and having Him take control of your life is simplicity personified, yet it's the most life-changing experience you could ever imagine.

(1) Tell God you're sorry for the way you have lived and you're willing to turn from your old ways: *"Lord, I'm so sorry for the way I have lived without you and deeply sorry for all my sins against you."*

(2) Say this prayer: *"Lord Jesus Christ, I know you stand at the door to my life and you've been knocking on it. I now open the door and ask you to come in. Take this life and glorify your Father with it. Thank you."*

Praise God. That's it!

Seek out a *Holy Spirit driven fellowship* as quickly as possible and talk to someone; tell them what you've done. Don't tell them about me; tell them about yourself and your conversion experience. Get baptised as soon as possible.

Now . . . God deals differently with each of those He loves and accepts. You may experience a gamut of bodily reactions from exhilaration to tears, shaking, uncontrollable laughter, or a simple peace without all those trimmings. Don't be afraid; that's the Holy Spirit being sealed in you. (You'll understand later. Don't run before you can walk.)

I thank God for you! I hope our paths cross one day—if not, they will in Heaven!

Barrie Kibble

<u>Notes</u>

<u>Notes</u>

Notes

Notes

Barrie Kibble

<u>Notes</u>

<u>Notes</u>

Printed in Great Britain
by Amazon